# Gree.. Country

## Vian Smith's

### Dartmoor and South Devon

## Introduced by Bob Mann

**Longmarsh Press**
**Totnes**

Published by Longmarsh Press 2009

5 Brook View, Totnes, Devon, TQ9 5FH, UK

www.longmarshpress.co.uk

ISBN 978-0-9561705-0-7

Printed and bound by Cpod, Trowbridge, Wiltshire

Cover picture: Dartmeet from the Coffin Stone by Barbara Kuyuate
Cover design by Gisele Afeche

# Acknowledgements

This book would not have been possible without the unconditional support, trust, generosity and commitment of Vian Smith's two youngest children and literary executors, Penney Long and Andrew Smith, who have helped in numerous ways, and have permitted me to use whatever I wanted from both his published and unpublished writings. I thank them sincerely, and hope they are pleased with the result.

Since I began exploring Vian's life and work, more than a decade ago now, I have received a great deal of help and interest from many people, especially those who knew him, who happily shared their memories or who loaned, and sometimes gave me, books, cuttings and pictures. Sadly, they did not all live to see this publication. Most important were his widow, Susan Smith, and his sister, Ruth Kasasian. Others for whom it appears too late are Bill Bennett, Bill Blinston, Rendle Crang, Ellen Mann, Janet Pryde and Fintan Rossiter. I am grateful for all the information and material they gave me, and am pleased to record their names here.

There are some I cannot even thank by name: the person who sent me a pristine copy of *Candles to the Dawn* after reading an article in the *Totnes Times*; the lady in Totnes Museum who remembered him on his first day at primary school, 'wearing a home-made purple suit;' and the one who lived near him in Sparrow Road in the late 1940s, and who told me she used to hear the typewriter late at night – for a moment I was back there with her, listening, in the cold street, over fifty years before.

Thanks also, for all kinds of help, to Gisele Afeche, Peter Cowlam, John Dumble, Maya Hussell, Walter King, Barbara Kuyuate, George Lidstone, Stuart MacDowall, Geoffrey Perring, Rod Richardson, J. Leon Robertson, Mike Smith, Ian Woodford, and to the staffs of the

Twentieth Century Archive Literary Collection at the University of Boston, Mass., and the Westcountry Studies Library, Exeter.

The introduction is based on articles which originally appeared in *Dartmoor - the country magazine* in Spring 2001, and *The Totnes Review* 2006, and I thank the respective editors for letting me recycle material from them.

Bob Mann
Totnes, December 2008

# Contents

## Sketches, Memories and Opinions

# VIAN SMITH

# An Outline of His Life and Work

*Bob Mann*

Lovers of Dartmoor tend also to be lovers of Dartmoor books, and any serious collection of these is likely to include, beside the classic volumes by Rowe, Crossing, Worth and the rest, Vian Smith's *Portrait of Dartmoor*, published by Robert Hale in 1966. Its author's best known work, this stands out from the other moorland tomes for the beauty of the writing and for his concern with the human experience of Dartmoor, rather than its scenic and wilderness qualities. In his distinctive, concentrated and passionate style, he argues for the needs of the moor's working inhabitants and weekend visitors, in refreshing contrast to the thin-lipped disdain often shown for both, certainly in those days, by preservationists.

Despite being more than twenty-five years out of print, the 'Portrait' is still fairly easy to find in second-hand bookshops, though judging from its non-appearance in bibliographies, it is rarely referred to by those who write about the moor today (which is their loss, and maybe why so much that is written is bland and predictable). But some readers, impressed by the individuality of his style and approach, may have wondered about the man behind it.

Vian Smith (it rhymes, by the way, with Brian, not Ian, and is *not* short for Vivian) died in 1969 at the early age of fifty, but he left over twenty books, including novels for adults and children, books about horses and horse racing, and a large amount of journalism, as well as plays for radio and television, short local guides and even a pantomime for his home town of Totnes. He was a working class Devonian who never, apart from his war service, lived more than a few miles from that home town, but through sheer effort and

1

determination he became a full-time professional author, with readers on both sides of the Atlantic; he saw some of his books translated into several European languages, and had his manuscripts collected by a major American university.

Since his death his works have mainly dropped beneath the horizon. Some Dartmoor enthusiasts will have his later novels set on the moor, and horse-lovers may still keep on their shelves his history of the Grand National, a book on point to point racing or his biography of a racehorse called Freddie. In general, though, you will have to search quite hard for any of these in second-hand shops and libraries.

Many long-term local residents will actually have read his work, years ago, without necessarily realising it; anyone who remembers a distinctive weekly newspaper published in Torquay in the 1950s and 60s, the long-defunct *South Devon Journal*, will have been exposed to hundreds, if not thousands, of articles, stories, prose-sketches and features that he wrote under various pseudonyms, as well as his own name. Indeed, according to one journalist who followed him, 'he set the whole tone of the paper.'

Vian Smith lives on in Totnes in the vivid memories of those who knew him, and his name no doubt comes up, occasionally, further afield, in the lunchtime reminiscences of ageing newspapermen who began their careers in South Devon. He was, clearly, like him or not (and some didn't), a person who could not easily be forgotten, whether as a lover of people and animals, a devoted family man or as a sportsman. He was radical in his views, and always a defender of the underdog and the vulnerable. But it is through his work that he deserves, ultimately, to be remembered, and, as we approach the fortieth anniversary of his death, it seems a good time to re-assess him. He is an important twentieth century regional writer, and one who is well worth rediscovering.

Reviewing the *Portrait of Dartmoor* in the *Mid Devon Advertiser*, Bernard Barnett, a former colleague, stated that with its publication, Vian Smith was no longer 'novelist and dramatist only,' but had earned 'the wider and more honourable title of writer.' He went on to suggest that, in the future, Vian might be remembered, with even more honour, simply as a 'Dartmoor writer.'

Dartmoor is certainly pivotal to his work, but so, too, are the gentler South Devon lowlands surrounding it. Growing up in Totnes, with its river and satellite villages, mellow old buildings, narrow streets and green lanes, not forgetting its infinitely graded social strata, was vitally important in forming his vision. Rather than seeing him purely as a Dartmoor writer, I prefer to think of his imaginative territory, his 'green country,' as embracing both the high moors and the red-soil landscapes below. Essentially it is Dart country; the river is the central thread, from the streams that begin high up in the bleak northern wastes, to the broad estuary he was born beside, and never lived far away from. Significantly, one of his favourite places was Dartmeet.

At its most characteristic, his writing expresses a deep understanding of this country and the experiences of human beings within it, living and working against an elemental environment that can never be a mere picturesque backdrop. We're rarely far from people working, and the work is basic, tough and unending, whether it is children picking flowers and berries for their mothers to sell in the market, or men dressed in sacks spreading muck on a grey January hillside. Like all the best country and landscape writers, he combines an appreciation of beauty which is at times almost visionary, with a simultaneous awareness of the reality of the struggle to make a living in a particular place, an awareness of the inseparability of joy and pain. This puts him in the company of those authors who, while remaining close to their native landscapes, manage to express something universal within the intensely local: R. S. Thomas in Wales, George Mackay Brown in Orkney, Ronald Blythe in East Anglia, Donald R. Rawe in Cornwall, Edward Storey in the Fens, and South Devon's own Brian Carter (whose background is remarkably similar to Vian's), as well as numerous others. At times he is with the best of them.

Vian Crocker Smith (all three are surnames: Vian is from Cornish ancestors on his father's side, and Crocker was his mother's maiden name) was born in Totnes on 2nd February 1919, at the family home in Mount View Terrace, a small row in the local brown stone near the edge of the old medieval town. His mother, Mary Smith, was active in local life, including amateur dramatics and the parish church. His father, Albert, was a master carpenter and cabinetmaker. They had one other child, Vian's younger sister Ruth.

He attended the two main primary schools in the town and sang in the church choir. His lifelong love affair with the moor began with visits to his maternal grandparents, who farmed at Langaford, near Holne, 'on the long climb from Buckfast Abbey.' In the 'Portrait' he recalled: 'I thought the moor was the Old Testament and that my grandfather was Abraham. It did not seem absurd that there might be a burning bush; that a voice might split the clouds, telling Abraham that the sacrifice was unnecessary, he could take the boy home now.'

His other great love, of horses and horse racing, also began early. In his last book, *Parade of Horses* (US title: *Horses in the Green Valley*), published the year after his death, he describes his adventures at Totnes Races and his memories of a small circus that regularly visited the town. Reading these and the other autobiographical chapters in that book, we can only regret that he did not live to give us a full account of his childhood; it would easily have rivalled *Cider With Rosie* or the reminiscences of Dylan Thomas, or, indeed, Brian Carter's memoir of his Paignton boyhood, *Yesterday's Harvest*. Perhaps because they appear in a book for younger readers about horses, interspersed with chapters on the history of humanity's relationship with that animal, and because he never mentions his home town by name, they have so far been overlooked. I hope the inclusion of three of them here brings them wider appreciation, not least in Totnes itself.

Vian was a born storyteller; his sister remembered listening to his early inventions as they lay in bed. Later he filled notebooks with stories and drawings. He sensed his vocation from an early age. Looking back in 1966 he stated that the two seminal moments in his life were being told by a teacher, at the age of eleven, that a piece he had written 'had something,' and seeing a display of his first novel in a London bookshop. The teacher, Mr Kinsman at Totnes Church Junior School, persuaded his parents to let him go on to the town's old-established King Edward VI Grammar School. It is interesting that the plot of *Press Gang* (1961), his novel of cut-throat journalism, and his last adult book not wholly concerned with horse racing or Dartmoor, hinges on loyalty to a primary school teacher.

4

At grammar school he excelled at subjects that interested him, like English and History, and ignored the ones that didn't, like Latin. He had had a slight speech impediment from early childhood, but was prevented from becoming too introspective by his love of sport. He played football for the school, and later the town; in fact, many older Totnes people I have spoken to remember him more as a footballer than as a writer.

In September 2002 the Old Totnesian Society, for alumni of the grammar school and its succeeding incarnations, included in its newsletter an essay called 'Devon's Beauty' which 'V. Smith' of Form 2B had published in the school magazine, *The Totnesian*, in the autumn term of 1932. It is possibly his first published work, and is not at all bad for a thirteen-year-old. Here is some of it:

An 'Ideal Dream' a well-known poet calls this fair county in a snug prosperous corner of the Mother-Land and judging by the number of pleasure-seeking hikers and cars laden with precious cargoes of humanity which are frequently seen in the countryside, the poet made little error.

This county, washed by continual waves on the North and South, is the magnet for city people who are anxious for a well-earned holiday and change from the continual bustle of dense crowds and the mocking roar of cars as they wend their way through the labyrinth of streets. Instead reposes the peaceful countryside, whose splendour is received with unbelievable welcome.

Some of these excited people may enjoy a quiet paddle down a rippling river - that forms part of Devon's beauty - with the clear trilling of the birds mingling with the soft strains of a banjo or gramophone.

On each side the rowers see sombre stately woods with the rich velvety grass rising up to meet the clear cloudless sky.

Another party would rather enjoy a brisk tramp, scanning with hungry eyes the beautiful countryside; and then, later, luxuriously lean back under the pleasant shade of a thatched roof inn, while devouring with marvellous rapidity the excellent fare of strawberries and cream and a tankard of Devonshire cider...

Is not Devon the Prince of beauty spots? No wonder the reputed poet called it the 'Ideal Dream.'

Perhaps he too, weary of life's toils and ups and downs, sought a refreshing place to rekindle his inspiration and, selecting Devon, met with success.

Unfortunately, I have been unable so far to identify the 'reputed poet.'

On leaving school, after a false start as an office boy in the Dartington Hall Gardens Department, a job he lost through taking time off to play football, he became apprenticed to a painter and decorator. This was, he reckoned, the least tiring of the building trades, and would leave him with the energy to write in the evenings. He was determined to become a writer, and it is worth remembering just how unattainable this would have seemed for a small-town, working class young man at the time, even after a few years at grammar school.

In 1939, whilst working for Staverton Builders, a job took him to Dorset, where he met his wife, Susan. They were to have five children. But first, there was the war.

He joined the army as soon as he could, and his experience over the next few years, with the Royal Engineers, gave him the subject for his first novel, *Song of the Unsung*, published by Hodder and Stoughton on 30th April 1945. Subtitled 'A Story of Sappers,' it describes the fall of France and the evacuation of Dunkirk as experienced by Vernon Lawrence and his companions. Lawrence is clearly a spokesman for the author, though noticeably of a higher social status. The *Totnes Times*, proudly reviewing it, told readers they would have no trouble recognising their own locality, and even their local paper.

The book sold reasonably well, and in the following year the sequel, *Candles to the Dawn*, appeared. This is more like a conventional first novel in that the theme is the hero's search for his identity. The war is over, and Lawrence, having decided to be a writer and painter, is pondering the person he wishes to become: 'He wanted to be quiet and free, kind and thoughtful... while watching the stars above the Rhine he had vowed to develop Vernon Lawrence and at the same time acquire the art of living gracefully and coherently.'

The book is one of my favourites amongst the early novels, and is full of insights into the young author's mind (we can reasonably assume that Lawrence's opinions are his own).

He lists his early reading:

Young England, Fifth Form at St Dominic's and David Copperfield... His later youth had been particularly troubled by conflicting opinions and

6

challenging morals. Michael Arlen, Shaw, H. G. Wells, Noel Coward, Phillip Gibbs and Sean O' Casey had wrestled within him... during the long winter evenings of his war years... he had read at random, Shelley, P. G. Wodehouse, Rose Macauley, Clifford Odets, John Steinbeck, Stephen Leacock and Duff Cooper.

Full of hope and the desire to build a better world, he vows that there will be no superficial cynicism after this war, as there had been after the last: 'no more cruel poems, slick novels or champagne plays.'

And there are glowing descriptions of his local countryside. Lawrence walks with his girlfriend, Flick:

Bound by mutual understanding, they continued beneath trees to the hill which fell down to the village. It lay in the valley, small and white, hugging the church like a litter of puppies... Slowly she turned from him and gazed towards the hills which cradled the valley in a protecting arm. Fields and woodlands lay at peace beneath a sun-flushed sky and the world stood still and looked in upon itself, like wine in a silver spoon.

Drawn into a village cricket match, Lawrence asks who they are playing, and is told it is Staverton, on the Dart:

Staverton, where in the gloom of trees, flowers gathered to discuss life as they lived it, where waters murmured a promise of secrets never fully divulged and in the cool evening, men and women wandered, red and shining from sun and wind, living slowly, their wealth the tired luxury of those who have worked. They were people of a deathless pageant, unobservant and unobserved, moving quietly against a cloth of colour, peace and eternal promise.

He cannot resist, however, a dig at Staverton's new mill, home of the builders he had worked for before the war: 'red and new, parent of mass-production, incredibly misplaced.'

For a while Vian, Susan and their growing family stayed in Totnes at his parents' home in Sparrow Road, while he worked at his novels. Later they moved to Rose Cottage in the Dartside village of Dittisham, at the time very much a working Devon community, harvesting a living from its river and orchards.

*Hungry Waters* and *The Hand of the Wind* appeared in February and August 1948. They tell the story of Adam Barnabas, a young man from a northern industrial city, who finds himself in Totnes (called 'Coombe Hazzard'), meets a girl and decides to settle nearby and seek fulfilment as a village craftsman – a dream that countless others have shared in the decades since then. The town and its life are lovingly described. Later, though, it all turns very dark, when Adam's wife has an affair and dies after an incompetent abortion carried out by an old woman in Plymouth, whose one-armed son is allowed to rape her the night before the operation (but not, most considerately, the night after).

Between 1945 and 1950 Hodder and Stoughton published seven novels by Vian C. Smith (he later dropped the initial). The number itself is impressive, showing his sheer energy and determination. Lots of people write and publish a novel during their lifetime; some go on and write more. For a very small number, it becomes the main occupation. Seven in five years is commitment, if nothing else, especially in that dark post-war period of housing shortages, rationing and disillusionment.

The novels themselves have sunk into the great ocean of lost books, but are worth fishing deeply to find. There is something about them that will always live: an attractive quality of respect and compassion for the lives of 'ordinary' people, especially women; a liveliness of observation and the general sense of a young writer revelling in the discovery of his talent. The landscapes and culture of Totnes and South Devon are ever present. Critics were encouraging, though some picked him up for the slightness of the plots, a certain mannered folksiness, and attempts at 'fine writing,' including an over-fondness for the use of simile.

The remaining three are *Holiday for Laughter* (1949), which has a hero with a stutter; *So Many Worlds* (1950), set partly in Dittisham: a pure wish-fulfilling fantasy about an idealist who is given a fortune and who tries to do good with it; and *Stars in the Morning* (1950), the first of his books in which horse racing becomes a major theme.

Things then became difficult. As he wrote in a 1956 article: 'Six years ago I walked into my Dittisham home; sat down to write; and had polio. Just like that... For about two years I carried the limp with me, and had to think twice about going upstairs.' He recovered, but his football playing was over. His editor at Hodder and Stoughton died, and he had to return for a while to painting and decorating. Mike Smith (no relation), a retired bricklayer from Totnes, remembers working with him on sites in Dartmouth and Totnes: 'He'd stand and paint the middle of the wall, and make the apprentice do the top and bottom.'

Perhaps to deal with his frustration at having to return to manual work, Vian wrote at this time a novel about men on a building site. The publishers, now without the editor who had championed him, rejected it. As one of the two or three people to have read it, I can see why. *Straw in Paradise* is not badly written; his style by now was honed and confident. It is just that there are no characters attractive enough for the reader to identify with or care about. They are exploited by an unfair system, but they are all so mean, cruel, selfish and dishonest that you cannot really give a damn. One, the site's cook, is a convicted paedophile, who is shown hanging around a scout camp and trying to pick up a seven-year-old on a beach. Challenging stuff for the time, just like his depiction of backstreet abortion and rape in *The Hand of the Wind*, but the publisher's reaction is understandable. Having got it all out of his system, Vian seems to have felt the same, as he never tried to place the book anywhere else, or re-use characters or incidents in later novels. In fact, he seems now to have drawn a line under all his early work, as his first seven novels are only listed in the front of one of his later books, and the middle 'C' disappears from his name.

The vehicle for his re-invention was a weekly newspaper called the *South Devon Journal*, published by the Devonshire Press in Torquay, and owned by George Lidstone. Nearly fifty years later, sitting with me in his spacious apartment overlooking Torbay, Mr Lidstone clearly remembered 'a rather slight man, with a limp and something of a stutter,' standing in front of him, asking for a job. And he got one.

Vian's entry into journalism was not, therefore, by the normal route of the time, that of being a 'cub reporter,' waiting in the rain outside a church to record the names of the mourners at funerals, or rushing to a phone box to get his story in before the opposition. He was already over thirty, and a published author. But then, he wasn't going to work for a normal kind of paper.

The *South Devon Journal* eschewed hard news for wholesome family reading and 'human interest' stories. Looking through old copies, the reader has the impression that the people of the towns and villages (it circulated throughout what is now Torbay, Teignbridge, the South Hams and Plymouth) are being addressed as one huge, extended family, and many of its features are those of a magazine rather than a newspaper. There are 'arty' pictures with elaborate captions, short stories, and many opportunities for readers to interact with their paper. It's a publication to be read slowly at leisure, passed around, kept and reread. The 'Journal' represented, in its ethos if not its content, the sort of popular journalism that was best exemplified at the time by Hugh Cudlipp's *Daily Mirror*, with its sense of being genuinely on the side of the people. It suited Vian perfectly, and he quickly made the paper his own, eventually becoming 'news editor' and staying for seven years. One fellow journalist told me: 'he created the paper in its golden age.' With a fluency that was the envy of everyone he worked with, he turned out articles, short stories, prose-sketches and dialect pieces, as well as straightforward reportage. He often, under various pseudonyms, wrote three quarters or more of the paper. Most of his Dartmoor pieces were by 'Rowley.' He was also 'Journeyman.' His Devon dialect stories were by 'John Britton.'

He seems, after a while, to have been given a remarkable amount of freedom. He did not even have to go into the office every day, but would do a lot of his writing at home. The photographer Stuart MacDowall, who provided the pictures for *Portrait of Dartmoor*, told me that he would collect Vian one or two mornings a week, and they would travel around South Devon, talking to people, picking up tips and ideas, finding stories wherever they went. Vian would sit with a notebook on his knees, writing constantly (he never drove himself, and those who knew him thought this was probably a good thing). One day, in Bovey Tracey, they found an elderly couple running a greengrocers' shop, whose broad Devon accents and lively interaction inspired Vian's imagination. They became 'Emmy and Fred,' who first appeared as characters in Totnes Pantomime, which he wrote in 1955 (by this time the family had returned to Totnes, and lived in Mansbridge Road, high up in Bridgetown; from here he could survey the whole

10

of his 'green country,' the old town below, the Dart valley, the moor on the skyline). The stories of Fred and Emmy became 'Journal' favourites, and the old couple were well enough known to be represented in local carnivals.

If it all sounds rather cosy to us today (it sounds pretty idyllic to me, actually), the daily experience of working for the 'Journal' seems to have been quite stressful, and a reporter who was there a little later than Vian, after reading my copy of *Press Gang* (ostensibly about a busy evening newspaper in a northern city), told me that the atmosphere of fear and tension he remembers are very much as Vian depicts them in the book. The novel reveals Vian's passionate commitment to the journalistic ideals he believed in, which he saw as in danger of being compromised (what he'd have said about the decline of the popular press, had he lived into the age of Maxwell and Murdoch, doesn't bear thinking about).

Nor were serious issues entirely absent from the 'Journal.' In a copy from 1956 I came upon an impassioned tirade under his own name against the church's failure to speak out against nuclear weapons: ' "Lighten our darkness," says the lamp outside the stark grey church of Lustleigh. But the lamp has no light to guide, only its shell remains; and there you have in little one of the tragedies of our time...'

At the end of the 1950s Vian started writing novels again, for both adults and children, and over the next decade his two great loves, Dartmoor and horses, came to dominate his work. His children rode from an early age, and he began to train his own racehorses, ridden by his middle son, Mark. He took the whole business very seriously, gaining a trainers' certificate from the Jockey Club, and racing his horses around the country. This was not an easy passion to indulge on a housing estate in Totnes; the horses were kept a few miles away, and an article about Vian and his life that appeared in a national paper describes him, early in the mornings, as walking briskly along the Newton Abbot road to see to them, before going to work.

His 1961 racing novel *Question Mark* (US title: *Pride of the Moor*) gives a sombre but beautiful portrait of life in a Dartmoor village, and a young man's attempt to break away from his background through sport (though the scene where a stallion's spirit is broken during the annual pony round-up is not for the squeamish; Vian hated all cruelty to animals, and doesn't spare us the reasons why; he once wrote that, while he loved racing, he also hated it for what it did to both people and horses).

A similar theme is explored in what is probably the best of his novels for young readers, *Horses of Petrock* (1965), set in a Westcountry racing stable; the American version, *A Second Chance*, is longer and deals more thoroughly with issues of generational and social tensions which are still relevant. He writes well for older children and teenagers, is never condescending, and gives them serious things to think about. But children's literature, then as now, was dominated by magic and time travel, and they received less attention than they deserve.

In his adult novels *Genesis Down* (1963), *The First Thunder* (1965) and *The Wind Blows Free* (1968) he deals convincingly with nineteenth century class conflict on Dartmoor, not a subject anyone else seems ever to have bothered to look at, in either fact or fiction. The best is *Genesis Down*, which is possibly, with the 'Portrait,' his masterpiece. It concerns the old custom of building a house in a day, a theme that obviously inspired his sympathy and imagination. Form, style and plot are beautiful brought together in a completely satisfying whole. Here are just a few of my favourite short passages and phrases from it:

The thatched house, long and squat and built of granite, had been made longer by additions... on the right was the cart shed, with red shafts peering out like the horns of a snail.

On the other side of the house, where the hand of the sun was like a blessing, Mrs Tamlyn had her garden and strawberries and beehives. The hives were of yellow straw, and around them the warm air trembled with a brown plotting.

When you've lived in an old house a long time, all your life, you know every shadow of it and every groan in it; then the house tells you what it hides from others. A closed door does not make a secret.

She gave furze to the fire, and the furze remembered another joke and crackled its laughter as the sparks went up.

The music almost ceased. It seemed to be smiling as a cat smiles in the sun.

The light in the window made its own world, like the inner light of a fire where the shapes and dreams are.

In October, with rust in the bracken and the cold singing, they went down the hill to the farm which had been their beginning.

He returned to the 'house in a day' idea when telling the story of Grannie Satterley in the 'Portrait,' and had already used it in the early tale 'House in a Day,' both of which are in this collection.

These novels sold better, and received more critical attention, in the United States than in Britain; it is strange to see reviews quoted on the dust wrappers from newspapers in Arizona or San Francisco, praising him for the truth of his evocation of the moor. My favourite describes his writing as having 'a haunting quality... as if the reader was once again entering a long-loved but temporarily forgotten scene.'

It was at about this time that Boston University started collecting his manuscripts for the Twentieth Century Archives Literary Collections, which has the aim of storing the papers of an eclectic range of 'novelists, essayists, poets, biographers and non-fiction writers,' with the object of 'documenting what was being written, what was being read and what was influencing public opinion from the turn of the century to the present.' The two or three hundred writers he shares the archive with include some of the great names of the century as well as those so obscure that only the most pedantic will have heard of them. One other Totnes writer is there as well: Mary Wesley.

After a period on the *Mid Devon Advertiser* in Newton Abbot, followed by a brief return to the 'Journal,' Vian gave up newspapers for the life of a full-time, free-lance author. In order to be close to the horses, the family moved to Netherton Farm, Littlehempston. This is a long, rambling old house, with many barns and outbuildings, in a narrow, enclosed valley not far from the famous haunted castle of Berry Pomeroy, and perhaps even within range of the castle's strange spell; I certainly felt haunted when I went there recently.

Sometimes he would disappear into the moor, where he would stay with his friends the Brackenbury family, who owned the Ring o'

Bells at North Bovey and also trained racehorses. After one extended visit to the pub, in 1965, he came back with the first draft of *Portrait of Dartmoor*.

The book was published the following year to immediate acclaim in the Westcountry and beyond. Even the TLS intoned its approval. But, typically, it aroused immediate controversy as well.

Describing the villages and towns around the moor, he makes plain his dislike of recent developments at Horrabridge, and says that the old bus drivers' name for it, 'Horror bridge,' has been revived, quite rightly in his view. The people of the village did not like this, and made their views known to the *Western Morning News*. When a reporter turned up at the door, Vian's laconic reply was 'It's just an opinion.'

The more I have learned about the man, the more I can see that the book is a portrait of himself as much as it is of the moor. When he has to merely present facts, like measurements of stream and tor, he is impatient, even perfunctory, but when a human story excites his imagination he is in his element. The book is nothing if not individual. The short chapter on sport, for example, covers hunting and horse racing, but nothing else. He frequently deplores the elitism of the National Park committee, and his defence of army training on the moor is, whether you agree with him or not, perfectly reasonable. He admits it is a nuisance, but points out 'there are worse offences than committing a nuisance,' and that 'committing to foreign service young soldiers who have not been thoroughly trained is one of them.' He had, after all, been in a war when he was twenty, which most of us have not. His dismissal of the Cranmere Pool mystique is equally his own.

Throughout the 1960s Vian wrote incessantly, producing sixteen books, five radio plays and two television plays, as well as continuing to write articles and features, and training his horses. It is exhausting just to think about, and clearly the strain was eventually too much. Four years after moving to Netherton, on the evening of 7th December, he collapsed and died of a heart attack, while visiting his beloved horses.

His funeral was held at St Mary's church, Totnes, where he had sung as a boy, then his body was cremated and his ashes scattered around the old Coffin Stone on the hill above Dartmeet, where generations of Dartmoor people, carrying their dead for burial at Widecombe, have stopped and rested.

This was one of his favourite places, where he would sit and ponder his current book. Apart from the sense of kinship and continuity with past ages, which would naturally appeal to his imagination (see page 50), it is an interesting, even illuminating, choice of location. The stone is not especially high up; you do not look down from it at a 'view.' You are in the landscape rather than above it. Unless you know exactly what you are looking for, the boulder itself is not easily distinguishable from the hundreds of others lying around. Sitting on it, you are inconspicuous. Though Yar Tor looms dramatically on one side, you can also see the trees of the valley where the waters of the two Darts come together. Cultivated fields and buildings are also visible. The road and its traffic are only yards away, sheep and ponies graze all around. The landscape is elemental but humanised. This is Vian's Dartmoor, not a separate, timeless wilderness, but a special place linked by river, road and history to the fertile meadows, villages and towns below. It is above all 'a place where people work and live.'

As mentioned earlier, there are still many people around who knew Vian, at all periods of his life. I have been impressed, in talking to them, by the vivid impression he obviously left on everyone, whether they liked him or not. Even the emphatic manner in which people have stated 'I knew Vian Smith!' is eloquent in itself. Here are just a few comments I have recorded:

'He was a rebel.'

'Prickly; a man's man, hanging around Newton Abbot racecourse in a trilby with a fag hanging from his mouth (Vian smoked fags, not cigarettes), or holding court to younger journalists in the pub at lunchtime.'

'He wasn't everybody's cup of tea, but I wouldn't like you to say anything derogatory about him.'

'A lovely man, but when he was in drink he could be nasty.'

'He used to walk around the lanes muttering to himself; that was how he created the dialogue for his plays and novels, literally saying it all out loud.'

'He could write anywhere. He always had a notebook in his hand, on the bus or wherever. He was constantly writing.'

Which brings us neatly back to the point of this book, his writings.

Vian approached the craft of writing in the same way as his father had approached his cabinet making, and he became as much a master of it. There was nothing of the isolated, superior artist about him; he was a working writer, doing what he hoped was a useful job. Some have regretted that horses and horse racing came to be such dominant themes, to the exclusion of other subjects, but he had to do what he was best known for. Once he left the newspapers, he needed to write whatever would pay the bills, and if this meant a pony series for a girls' comic, or a piece about lambing for a women's magazine, or the biography of a racehorse, that's what he wrote. Like all real artists he used what was in front of him, in his life, just as the Dartmoor hill farmer had used the stones he found lying around on the moor for his walls. Vian's horses, and the family life built around them, gave him a ready-made and inexhaustible subject. At this time he also turned some of his books and ideas into plays for radio and television, and though I have not been able to study these, I once came across a letter to him from some neighbours who had watched one of his plays. They had, they said, become so absorbed in the story that they totally forgot they were only watching it because they knew the author. Maybe a slightly back-handed compliment, but one that any writer would actually be delighted with.

I have not tried to cover the whole of Vian's career in this collection. There is nothing from his novels or children's books, and racing only features in the childhood reminiscences. This is Vian the Devonian and countryman, the journalist and craftsman of letters. I wanted my choice to reflect the complexity and seriousness of his engagement with the life of his home area, and his inside knowledge of it, but also his joyful celebration of place, his pure pleasure in playing with words, his sportsman's keen sense of occasion and physicality (I get the impression he was very sensitive to the cold)), and, not least, his appreciation of good country food and drink.

His prose style is distinctive and, once the reader is used to it, the rhythms and cadences are instantly recognisable. Some of the early journalism, like the early novels, may seem, today, rather flowery and old-fashioned. It is the sort of writing that critics of the time were beginning to look at with frowning disapproval. Prose, they said crossly, was just not meant to be like this (nor, according to some of them, was poetry). The discipline imposed by writing for newspapers, of having to say everything in so many words and no more, helped him to control the exuberance, teaching him how much could be implied without being overtly stated (journalism is much closer to poetry in this than many practitioners of the latter art might care to admit). By the time of *Portrait of Dartmoor* and the autobiographical chapters of *Parade of Horses*, even in such short articles as the two, included towards the end of this book, contrasting the bringing in of the harvest with how it all begins, eight months earlier, in the cold fields, he had cut and polished his style to a luminous perfection of concision and clarity that is equal to the best writing of its time.

Not everyone thought so, of course. As late as *The Grand National* (1969), at least one critic was offended by his habit of 'lapsing into schoolgirl rhetoric when he hasn't very much to say.' The passage in question is a description of the approach to Aintree: 'Where there are no houses, only spaces like memories of war, there is grass. The grass is long and pale. It weeps down the embankments, mourning the mugs who will lose today.'

You can see the reviewer's point, though in the context I think the image works well enough. If you accept the right of language to be colourful, and for art to occasionally draw attention to its artiness, then Vian's writing will give endless pleasure for its liveliness and lyrical flow (and it is interesting that he did express himself in this manner, considering the 'prickly,' impatient, very 'male' image conveyed by the comments from those who knew him). The danger of having a recognisable voice is always that, on a bad day, it can sound like a parody of itself, and Vian was no more immune to this than anyone else. I am confident, however, that there are no bad days in this collection.

I hope the extracts from *Portrait of Dartmoor* will encourage those who have not read it to go and look for a copy, and those who have it on their shelves to take it down again and revisit the whole work. I have chosen sections which are most uniquely his, especially the ones where he deals with the human history of the moor in the nineteenth and twentieth centuries.

Readers coming to his account of hill farming may be surprised at the amount of enclosure that occurred on the moor. The received wisdom is that the early nineteenth century Parliamentary enclosures, the cause of so much suffering and disruption in many parts of the country, did not affect Devon, because our fields and boundaries were made centuries before, in a much slower and steadier fashion; we have all the ancient hedges and banks and deep lanes to prove it. True, for the Devon lowlands, but on Dartmoor the process was as devastating as anywhere in the South or Midlands; there was just no Dartmoor John Clare to record the heartbreak. Yet I cannot think of another Dartmoor author who even glances at the subject.

The account of the prison mutiny is taken from his much longer chapter on Sir Thomas Tyrwhitt's creation of Princetown, and shows his ability to tell a story and create an atmosphere with a few deft strokes.

The earlier Dartmoor pieces, most of them by Rowley in the 'Journal,' are, I think, as fresh as when they were written. His knowledge of moorland farm life, inherited from generations on his mother's side, is clear. His sympathy with those living and working on the moor, as opposed to those who merely wish to preserve it, is refreshing, as is his lack of wilderness romanticism. His understanding of folklore, and how it continually re-invents itself, is deep and surprisingly contemporary, considering that, at the time, the subject was mainly the preserve of eccentric maiden ladies and vicars obsessed with pagan 'survivals' and fertility rites. His dislike of the National Park, or at least of those who ran it and spoke for it in the 50s and 60s, is undisguised (whether he would be any happier today is a good question; I can just imagine his reaction to the 'Please Take Moor Care' signs that greet us on every cattle grid).

The dialect Fred and Emmy stories, on the other hand, unlike most of his journalism, do not date so well, and I have not included any; the old couple do appear briefly, however, in the almost-Dickensian 'The Settle and the Screen,' just for the sake of completeness. His use of Devon dialect in other articles feels very natural and unaffected; it was, after all, his native speech. And his fondness for simile stayed with him to the end, as much a part of him as an unconscious gesture.

It could be that, in the future, the Longmarsh Press will be able to publish complete editions of the *Portrait of Dartmoor* and some of the novels. Meanwhile, I hope this anthology of shorter writings will serve as a sampler and whet the appetite for more. The title, though I use the term 'Green Country' to describe Vian's particular imaginative landscape, and he slips it into the circus chapter of *Parade of Horses*, is actually taken from a manuscript collection of stories and sketches he put together in the 1950s, now held by the Twentieth Century Archive in Boston. Some of the pieces later appeared in newspapers and magazines, but others are published here for the first time.

## A Note on Sources and Text

I have interfered with Vian's words as little as possible. On the occasions where he uses 'men' or 'man' to refer to the whole of humanity, I have quietly updated him to reflect today's sensibilities. All extracts from *Portrait of Dartmoor* are from the original 1966 edition, rather than from those with revisions by Gordon Dumble which Hale regularly re-printed until 1982; these were necessary when it was being presented as a contemporary portrait, but now, over forty years later, it would be impossible to update all the information without losing the character of the book altogether. Thus we have War Department rather than Ministry of Defence, pre-decimalisation monetary values and miles instead of kilometres.

Vian had a tendency to use a semi-colon where most of us would choose to put a comma; this can give his prose a slightly nervous, hesitating movement (though it was obviously acceptable to his editors). Where it works I have left it; where I think it impedes the flow a little too much, I have substituted a comma.

I have resisted the temptation to add my own comments describing all the changes which have taken place, especially on the moor, since Vian wrote about the area so vividly, as this information is readily available elsewhere. No one reading that a preservation society 'insisted' in 1966 that the line between Totnes and Ashburton could be reopened needs to be told that this successfully happened, at least as far as Buckfastleigh, or, for that matter, that the hill farm is probably now an executive's weekend retreat. But I have sometimes introduced a piece where I consider it useful, as with the guides to Totnes and Dittisham, and made the occasional, italicised, comment.

The sources given for articles and stories are those from which I have actually taken them. Therefore 'House in a Day' is from the MS 'Green Country,' although I am aware that it later appeared in the *South Devon Journal*. Abbreviations used are: GC (Green Country), SDJ (South Devon Journal), MDA (Mid Devon Advertiser) and WR (Woman's Realm).

# *Dartmoor*

# From **PORTRAIT OF DARTMOOR**

## The Land of Thunder

Dartmoor is granite country; an area of about three hundred and thirty square miles in the heart of Devon, reaching from Okehampton in the north to Ivybridge in the south (twenty four miles); from Ashburton in the south-east to Lydford in the north-west (eighteen miles) [*the National Park actually covers 365 square miles, but Vian had little time for the National Park*]. It was the source of tin and copper. It is the source of fourteen rivers which supply towns and cities near its border. It has given part of its character to a prison.

Dartmoor used to be called the 'Land of Thunder;' a name given by the people of border villages who looked up to the growling clouds and watched the weather grow. Recently the BBC called it 'The Last Wilderness.' It has also been called an 'irreplaceable document' of life since the early Bronze Age; a 'heritage' of wild land; an area where ancient rights are so preserved that hill farmers continue to graze cattle, sheep and ponies in the fashion of the thirteenth century; a military training area; and since 1951 a National Park, with the declared purpose of ensuring that the heritage is made available to all, including those of future generations.

But no one designation is enough. The truth is that Dartmoor has become many things to many people. The archaeologist reads history in its stones. The hill farmer uses it to graze stock. The War Department needs its heather miles to train gun-crews. Society uses a corner of it as a place of confinement for convicted criminals. The

23

people of Devon towns and cities turn their weekend cars towards its sense of freedom. Summer tourists from other parts of the country need its open spaces to escape Coronation Street and Park Lane.

So many purposes are not to be reconciled. The walker wants the lonely miles where gunfire flags are sometimes flying. The archaeologist wants every stone preserved for careful examination. The angler for trout and salmon wants silence. Those who have recently retired to moorland villages want privacy. The hill farmer defends his rights against gradual encroachment; while the National Park Committee, meeting once a month at Exeter, wants all to understand what they have inherited. Weekend cars and tourists want only to be left alone.

A result is confusion and often ill temper. Dartmoor, once a neglected wilderness, has become a cherished place. The pity is that it is cherished for so many reasons; many of them selfish and arrogantly expressed.

My own prejudice is that Dartmoor is not only a graveyard of history; nor primarily a quiet corner for the retired. It is what it has always been; a place where people work and live. I see the history of Dartmoor in terms of people and it is in those terms that this portrait is painted.

It is meant to be a portrait at three levels; Dartmoor as a rich museum, each detail strengthening the link between the people of the present and the people of the past; Dartmoor as a National Park, to which thousands can come for the healing simplicities of picnics in the heather and long views from the tors, for the evening ritual of watching the sun go down; and Dartmoor as an area of hill-farming, where men and women live on ancient rights.

# The Hill Farmer Through Two Centuries

Before 1772 the Dartmoor hill farmer was a man alone. Change had not reached him. His methods were those of his fore-fathers. His standards were their standards. He wore a long, loose blouse of thick blanket. His leggings were of fustian and his proudest possessions were his boots. They had been made by the cordwainer of a border village. Their iron plates had been added by the blacksmith. They had double flaps above the lace-holes to keep the water out.

His house was on the side of the hill, where the stream ran down to boulders at the bottom. It faced south. Its back was protected by the hill. It seemed to be hunching its shoulders. He did not know that when Bronze Age men had built their huts up on the moor, they had also built in the shelter of hills with the doorway facing south.

His house had one door, one window. The walls were five feet high and the roof was steep. The door was wide enough for animals. The animals turned left as they went in, occupying a windowless darkness on the left of a partial partition. The family kitchen was on the right. Their furniture was a table, two chairs and a dresser. The floor was thick with bracken, renewed each year and trodden tight for warmth and comfort. Steps led to the upper storey and the steps were stones protruding from the wall. There could not be a staircase because stairs meant wood and there was little wood on Dartmoor.

The upper storey was in two sections; the larger as a bedroom for the family, the smaller as a loft for storage. The cattle were fed from there when snow leaned on the house.

There were two beds; one for the parents, the other for the children. There were four children. The man was lucky for three of them were sons. The oldest was ten and old enough to gather stones and carry water and to milk and shear.

His patches of cultivated land were cut into the hill. He did not till for profit. He tilled to supply his family. Rye was for bread to be baked in the ashes; rye straw was for thatching. He also grew potatoes and turnips. Hay was for his stock in winter.

The earth was shallow but good. His patches were enclosed by walls, not only to establish possession but to protect young growth from wild weather. In this also he was following the pattern set by agriculturists of the late Bronze Age. He built the walls of granite, using the stones which littered the moor. He chose the stones for their sizes and availability; unaware that he was raiding kistvaens, the burial places of three thousand years ago; unaware that a hundred years later shrill protests would condemn him vandal.

He used what he could because there was nothing else. He built by setting long stones in a ground line with massive stones at the corners. Then he levered others into position so that each joint was tied. The walls were four feet high, with holes to leak the wind through. His newest walls seemed perilous, but those which had been built years ago had grown a skin of moss and lichen with tufts of course grass growing apparently from nothing.

His sheep were on the hill opposite. His ponies, the oldest animals of the moor, were hock deep in bracken; their heads always down in perpetual scrounging, only the flick of their tails making them alive. His cattle were limited to the number which he could feed in winter. Each April they were driven to their summer lair, where the grazing was best. They remained there until the autumn drift, when all animals were driven off the moor and claimed and sold.

His enemy was winter. He spent seven months of each year recovering from the last and preparing for the next. The man was afraid of winter because of his stock. His wife was afraid because of the children.

There was no consumption here nor diphtheria nor other city diseases. But there was whooping cough. The mother wrapped her child warm and carried him to where the night sheep had been lying. She placed the child in the form left by the sheep and he breathed in the smell. Only the smell of sheep could break the cough and save him. The other dreaded disease was measles. Then the fire could not be built high enough, the child kept warm enough. She wrapped him in her own warmth, frightened that after measles there would be blindness.

This clever woman knew what to do in an emergency. She rubbed salt into a cut to prevent infection; wrapped thick cobwebs around a cut to stop bleeding, She had a mixture of fat and sulphur for deep bruises; brown paper soaked in melted tallow and cut in the shape of a heart, for pain in the chest. But there were times when prayers and implicit belief in old remedies was not enough. Two of their children died and were carried across the moor to Widecombe, there to be buried in unmarked graves because they were poor people.

They seldom moved far beyond the hills which enclosed them. They saw only the Moorman, appointed by the Duchy of Cornwall to ride this quarter of the moor and to supervise the welfare of stock on common land. The coming of the Moorman was a great event, for he brought news and they were always hungry for news. One day he brought the news that the road across the moor from Moretonhampstead to Tavistock was not rumour merely. An Act had been passed. Soon work would begin.

But at that time they did not guess what the road would do. They continued to cut peat and burn heather, to bake bread and thrash rye. Once a year the man sold sheep and cattle; mongrel ponies for working in city streets. Sometimes he hoarded wool, waiting for a better price. Meanwhile work on the road began. Part of it was contracted by an old Moorman named Carter, who lived in a hut near Rundle Stone and had the services of his sons.

Still the hill farmer did not guess what the road would do. He continued to use pack-ponies; carrying dung to the fields in pots suspended from crooks on either side of a pony's back. He dragged stones down the hill by sledge. In July he cut peat for winter fires; in February or early March he burned a part of his grazing ground, burning old growth to set the new free. His way of life was hard and frugal. He and his family had nothing which they did not make themselves.

The road was finished. The way was open to change and the first change was the introduction of wheeled transport. The first carts appeared on the moor. These carts made the road a way out to the markets of Tavistock and Moretonhampstead. But the road was not only a way out. It was a way in for new men, new ideas. The new ideas needed land.

The first new man was Mr Gullet, who in 1780 began to improve the standard of farming at Prince Hall. He was succeeded by Sir Francis Buller, who extended the estate to two thousand acres. In 1785 Mr Thomas Tyrwhitt chose a sheltered corner of the moor and built Tor Royal as an ambitious farm. The new word was 'enclosure.'

Then the hill farmer realised. His cattle could not be driven to their lair for summer grazing. Their summer lair had been taken into private ownership. New walls had been built. Ancient rights had been suddenly denied. By 1810 vast quantities of the best land had passed from common to private ownership. The motives were always to improve agriculture and to create pockets of comparative prosperity. The effect was always to rob men of the rights on which they were dependent. In August 1898, Mr Seale Hayne was told in the House of Commons that since 1820 more than fifteen thousand acres had been enclosed on Dartmoor.

Early farmhouses on Dartmoor were different from moorland cottages only because the ground floor was divided by a partial or complete partition to make a place for cattle. Generations extended and improved the original structure. A stone wall screened the hearth from the main door, and this developed into a kind of lobby. It supported a partitioning of rooms above, making smaller rooms which ultimately incorporated the loft. What had been the place for storing fodder became a bedroom; what had been the place for animals became the parlour.

A shippon was built for animals, sometimes against a side wall of the house with a separate entrance; sometimes completely removed, yet not so far that the farmer could not reach his stock in winter. The main entrance was improved and sheltered by a deep porch. It had a floor of slate and a stone seat along each wall. There the family sat of a summer evening, facing each other, their knees almost touching, like passengers in a railway carriage.

An extension at the back or side, with access from the kitchen, became the dairy, while as a precaution against fire the men built a round ash-house thirty yards away. Ashes and embers were taken from the hearth each night and emptied into the ash-house through a hatch. Two hundred years later these round buildings were to be described as 'pixie houses' because Dartmoor women had forgotten their first use.

By 1850 the Dartmoor farmhouse was comparatively spacious and comfortable; each kitchen with a wide hearth for iron pots, each with a settle drawn between fire and door to block the draughts. The settle was high and straight of back. It was an evening place, and the sense of privacy which it afforded was as important as the fire. Families sat on its narrow bench, making the firelight a kind of stage. Father had his place in one corner, mother had the other. The children sat between and were told not to fidget. A sign of imminent adulthood was the ability to touch the stone floor with your toes.

Later generations removed thatch and substituted slate, thereby banishing the chronic fear of fire. They brought builders from a border town to plaster stone walls and to build new stairs; sometimes retaining the eccentric beams, less because they were picturesque than because of what might fall down if they were dragged out. Women wanted higher, wider windows; cement floors in scullery and dairy; cupboards made of recesses on stairs and landings. Lighting was by oil lamp, with candles for the bedrooms. Water was drawn from a well. Coal and wood were preferred to peat because peat made 'bistle' and 'bistle' defied the women's new pride in cleanliness.

The parlour became the best room and was used rarely. Its furniture was mahogany. The table was covered by a red cloth with tassels. The chairs had fixed positions and never seemed to move. It was used only for dinner on Sunday, or to receive relatives at a time of funeral or wedding.

The men wanted more shippons and barns, and built them in a rough square. Stones were split for the space in the middle and this became the yard. It was often between the house and the way in, so the gate to the yard became the first entrance to the house. The dog was barking long before you reached it.

Pack ponies and sledges continued to be used for farm work because carts could not operate in winter without a stone track. The hill farmer was reluctant to devote time and labour to the making of this track, but ultimately he built it and the way was open for carts and traps, for horses trotting home from market.

It was improved by succeeding generations, so that now there is a good road rising to the farm on the hillside.

The house cannot be recognised. Only if you look closely can you see the great slabs of granite which were the corner-stones. The yard gate is of tubular metal, the yard of concrete. The stone walls of the porch have been covered by a skin of sanded cement. But the slate floor is still there. So are the stone benches where the family sat in summer. The main door is of oak, studded with heavy nails like a crucifixion. It looks old, but it is not. In the first place it has a letter box. In the second it opens easily, swings readily, and the doors of the early nineteenth century never did. It has been made to seem old in tribute to the generations who built this house from nothing.

The hill farmer is proud of those generations, confessing that they showed greater ingenuity with stone and beam than ever he could manage. Yet he is proud, also, of the innovations which he has introduced; mains water and electricity, television, washing machine, refrigerator; signs of an affluence which makes his forefathers poorer by contrast. He thinks they must have been tough men, brave men. He knows they were betrayed men; betrayed by the acts of enclosure which snatched the best land. This bitterness is part of his inheritance. It explains his suspicion of change, his resentment of any further restriction or encroachment.

The hill farmer is a stock man. He does not grow corn or milk big herds. He breeds cattle, sheep and ponies. His black cattle are Galloways; his sheep are white-face Dartmoor. They are superior to the stock his forefathers owned, and this superiority is another kind of prosperity, made possible in part by price reviews, by subsidies and by the Agricultural Act of 1947. He will not admit this, for that act was a Socialist measure and he is anti-Socialist. He acknowledges help only from the Act of 1957, which amended and improved the first and was a Conservative measure. In this deeply rooted suspicion of Socialism, dating from the threatened introduction of trade unionism following Joe Arch's establishment of a National Union of Agricultural Labourers in 1872, he is sincere. Yet he has assimilated Socialist ideas, including subsidies and marketing boards and the National Health Service, into his way of life, and has forgotten their political origins.

He belongs to the National Farmers' Union with his colleagues of the border farms, but there is a subtle gulf between the hill farmer and his colleagues in the fertile valleys. The hill farmer needs to be less skilful, less steadily industrious. He needs to employ less labour, to invest in fewer implements. But the quality which most distinguishes him from the valley farmer is his pride in deep tradition. He does not often talk about it, but it shows; especially in his anger when his rights are threatened.

His wife is tall and efficient and reads *Woman's Realm* and watches 'Doctor Finlay's Casebook.' She bakes bread and makes wine in the old-fashioned way, but only for exhibitions organised by the Women's Institute. She has never made butter or cream or carried eggs to the pannier market. Butter is delivered with the tinned peas and tinned meats; cream is neglected as an over-rated delicacy; eggs are collected by the packing station. Her methods of keeping hens and selling eggs are vitally different from the way followed by her mother.

A generation ago the hens roamed the yard, scrounging fungi on the manure heap, scratching corners of grass. They perched at dusk among the carts of the linhay, and they laid in secret places, often among nettles. The farmer's wife was supposed to know where each hen was laying, for each egg was a penny or perhaps three-halfpence. Every morning she gathered the eggs and once a week she carried them to market by branch-line train. There she had her customers whom she called her 'regulars;' and the selling of a dozen eggs to each was a series of little ceremonies.

Now the hens are kept in deep litter; a long, low hut with cobwebbed windows for light and wood-shavings for scratching. They are persuaded to lay in darkened boxes and the eggs roll down to a compartment, making collection clean and easy. They never see the sun, never scratch grass; neither are they ever cold and wet, hunched up in rain like mourners. Their life-span is seldom more than eighteen months, after which they are sold for table and new pullets are brought in. This new efficiency is contemptuous of the old muddle, when miscellaneous hens were allowed to lay secretly or seldom, pecking the door to beg bacon-rind in the porch.

31

But prejudice persists. Many women in market towns prefer to buy eggs produced by hens on 'free-range;' meaning hens allowed to roam the grass and scuffle in dust-holes. The hill farmer's wife would not promise this, so the pannier market ceased to be her means of selling. Somebody else took over the market stall and the hill farmer's wife was relieved, for selling at the pannier market meant cold feet and mittens and the boredom of waiting for the regulars to show.

Her day-out is still Tuesday or Wednesday, but now she drives to Exeter for a hair-do, to Plymouth for the shops. The car is her own and she drives it fast; a more competent driver than her husband. She seldom buys at the village store. Weekly provisions come by vans from the border towns. She should have more leisure than had her mother, but she has not. The time once taken by making hogs-pudding and collecting eggs and carrying water is absorbed now by dental appointments and open-days and social dinners and committees. She belongs to many organisations, but not to the Mothers' Union or Sewing Guild or Wives' Circle or to any organisation sponsored by the church. She attends evensong three times a year and is always in a hurry.

Every October she is afraid. It is then that she buys wholesale; maintaining supplies of sugar, tea, flour, yeast, tinned foods, candles, paraffin against the threat of winter. She knows that winter can mock this modern façade and break through to the essentials. In 1963 it did.

Her farm was isolated for five weeks, completely snowed in for three. No mains water, no electricity, no vans or telephone. The hill farmer's wife went back overnight from the world of hair-do and Women's Institute to the lamp and candles of another generation. She bucketed water from the well and boiled it. She baked bread; made stews and broths; fulfilled the first essential of keeping her family fed and warm and dry. Meanwhile her husband and son dug a path from shippon to stream, breaking ice so that the calves could drink. They dragged hay to cattle and ponies, using a sledge in the fashion of the eighteenth century. They dug sheep from drifts and dragged them to shelter, there to dose them with whisky or brandy. Then they came to the fire and listened to the transistor, which had become their only contact with the world. The radio was announcing the distribution of hay to animals of the moor. The RSPCA was using helicopters, and the criticisms declared or implied that Dartmoor farmers were neglecting their stock.

The hill farmer's bitter resentment of the RSPCA, and similar organisations, dates from that time. He recognises that many of the criticisms were justified, that sheep and ponies died although reports were exaggerated; yet he cannot forgive those organisations for presuming themselves alone in their distress or for using an emergency to the advancement of propaganda. He suspects that a motive was less to protect the animals of the moor than to secure publicity.

In the spring of that year he watched the moor recover. It was a magical process. One week the snow seemed permanent, frozen as hard as concrete. By the next a slow thaw had reduced the level of the moor, so that what had been an erratic line of stones became two deep, three deep, showing where the wall would be if the thaw continued. Streams and rivers took away the thaw and the tattered hawthorn tree climbed out of its grave and the boulders came back and the gorse and heather until one morning the moor was brown again. The hill farmer saw then what had been done by the most severe snow since 1891. He was frightened, for it seemed impossible that the moor would ever fully recover. It was as barren as the dead.

Yet soon, incredibly soon, the moor was fighting back. There was movement where there had been nothing; signs of green where it had seemed nothing could be green again. Within a month the moor was alive. Lambs born in this period were incredibly strong. Animals which had been haggard were responding to the magic and the birds were back.

In May life on the moor was the same as in any other May. Mares were dropping their foals in the secrecy of night. Sheep were leading their lambs to high ground in the twilight of each day. Cattle were grazing, as still as though carved from black cardboard. The hill farmer looked out and felt the moor growing young and understood the relief, the gratitude which old country-dances and old country-songs had expressed.

# The Prison and the Mutiny

In 1909 William Crossing, most dependable of Dartmoor historians and seldom inclined to exaggeration, called Princetown the 'Capital of Dartmoor,' a high honour for Tyrwhitt's settlement of inn, mill and half-a-dozen cottages. It had succeeded Lydford as the headquarters of the Duchy of Cornwall.

Now its main street is wide, like a frontier town; an impression enhanced in summer by mares with foals at foot roaming along it. The oldest building is the 'Plume of Feathers,' the shops are brightly painted and on sunshine days it is possible to forget the grim history all around. But to come here in winter is to understand what life in Princetown has been about since Cornish masons fought the weather in 1805 *[when the prison, for French and American Prisoners of War, was built; it closed in 1816, and reopened as a convict prison in 1850]*.

February, according to Dartmoor tradition, is the month for snow; but January is the coldest month. November is the wet month, when mist clings to your lashes and seeps into your shoulders. You understand then why the wives of prison warders count the years of service; why children born here look to Plymouth as a way out; why released prisoners, remembering their years of confinement, remember not deep snow or wild storm but this seeping greyness.

The prison has been called 'the worst in England.' In 1927 Sir William Joynson-Hicks, then Home Secretary, called it a 'cesspool of humanity.' For more than fifty years there has been a smouldering campaign to have it closed. Recently those pressures promised to be soon successful, and Princetown came face-to-face with what its future would be without the prison as its purpose. The mask of hypocrisy slipped. Princetown saw again the threat of locked doors and empty cottages, of grass again in its streets. The fear of going back to 'Prince's Town' was behind its relief when the decision to transfer the prisoners was postponed.

Life within the prison has changed gradually, almost imperceptibly, since the middle nineteenth century when groups of 'agriculturists' began to drain the bogs. But in two respects life is identical to 1813. Prisoners are still preoccupied by food and tobacco.

Captive seamen in 1813 chewed rope, wood and leather as substitutes for tobacco. Prisoners now, like the Americans then, think about tobacco, covet tobacco, gamble tobacco. The aristocracy are 'Tobacco Barons' who are bookmakers and currency-lenders yet more than that. Their power pervades, although it has been alternately exaggerated and denied. To be heavily in debt to the 'Tobacco Barons' is to go in fear. Such fear explains why men, with only short periods still to serve, make hopeless dashes from working parties. These attempts are not planned. They are doomed to failure. Yet they are not without a purpose.

The purpose is to escape the 'Tobacco Barons,' for it is the unwritten law among prisoners that an attempted escape wipes out all debts. The sacrifice of remission is a price paid for a kind of safety within prison society.

An ex-prisoner, telling of this preoccupation with tobacco, showed me how a prisoner rolls a cigarette. The thread of tobacco; the expert flick of the paper; a precise and delicate licking of the gummed edge. He showed me how a prisoner lights it; by scratching a split match on granite, then by leaning so close that the quickest spark is enough. The paper burns in a red eye. It reaches the tobacco and he drags in the smoke with a hunger and concentration known only to the deprived. He uses every shred of the cigarette. If he is interrupted or detected his reaction is immediate. He swallows it.

To this ceremony of illicit smoking the vestas match is important; and for the making of a supply of matches he has a tool furtively made and carefully sharpened. It might be the corner of a razor blade, set in wood and small enough to be concealed in a hand. It could be used as a weapon. But its primary function is to slice the red-tipped match so that each sliver of wood has a red tip.

I knew a man who boasted that he could make sixteen matches out of one; but when I watched the operation he managed only twelve.

Food is important less because the men are hungry, than because the allocation of food is an allocation of 'rights' and every prisoner learns to be sensitive about his 'rights.' In 1810 the French demonstrated against the quality of bread. The spark which lit the 'American Massacre' of 1815 was an attempt to impose a ration of biscuit instead of bread. In 1932 the fuse to the mutiny was again protests about food.

There were other grievances at the time; including changes of rules which seemed reasonable to administrators but which repressed men who clung to routine as to a kind of sanity. But the expressed grievance on 22nd January 1932 was the quality of the breakfast porridge.

The Governor, Mr S. N. Roberts, examined it and agreed that it was not properly cooked. He ordered an extra ration of bread, potatoes and margarine. The following day the porridge was again suspect. The Governor, persuaded that water had been maliciously added, judged it to be 'eatable' but issued four ounces of corned beef instead. On the same day at chapel he apologised for the repeated failure of the porridge and added: 'I am anxious to see you get fair play.'

Perversely some of the prisoners interpreted this as weakness; as seventy years before other prisoners had rejected attempts to introduce humane reforms. They refused to sing the chapel hymn and the chaplain sang it alone. Experienced officers, always nervous at chapel-time when prisoners come together and the mischief of ring-leaders can run like heather fire, knew that it was coming. The feeling of mutiny coloured the air like the yellow light before a storm. All Princetown felt it. Traders and workmen and their wives looked towards the grey buildings and waited for the silence to explode.

Shortly after nine o'clock on Sunday morning, 24th January the silence exploded and for two hours all the prison, except the gates, was commanded by mutineers. Stones were thrown. Pick-shafts became weapons. So did nails tied in cloths. Windows were smashed, including every pane of glass in the Wesleyan chapel. Its minister, the Reverend F. S. Scholes, was assaulted; but when he lost his spectacles in the scuffle a mutineer stooped for them and returned them with apology.

Offices were wrecked. As a prelude to arson the fire engine was smashed. Clocks were broken. The Church of England chapel and vestry were ransacked. But the mood of the mutineers changed when at last they found the cigarettes. Rejoicing at sudden abundance they gave away cigarettes, even offering one to the Medical Officer who accepted it.

Men danced. Someone sang. Others put on officers' caps and coats and applauded themselves. The popular song was 'I'm Dancing with Tears in my Eyes.' But there was no mass assault on the gates, no determined attempt to break out.

The officers' first responsibility was to prevent a mass break-out; their second was to prevent a repeat of the 'massacre.' They patrolled outside the boundary walls, armed with revolvers and with Snider rifles loaded with buckshot. They fired as men appeared on the roofs. A leader was wounded and the ugly cry went up: 'They got one of ours – murder them.' But still the anticipated break-out did not come. Ring-leaders seemed to be fascinated by their power to destroy. Their easiest weapon was fire.

Smoke billowed from the administration block; making a symbolic pyre of authority. Dartmoor families hurried to the hills and looked through the grey morning to smoke as ominous as a volcano. After nearly one hundred years they had become accustomed to the convict prison; to the brief tension of occasional escapes and to the old fears of finding themselves face to face with desperate men. This Sunday morning they realised fully what might happen if the rifles were not enough; if the gates opened and if the most dangerous criminals in modern society were suddenly free.

Thirty police of the Plymouth city force, strengthened by others of the county force, came into Princetown. They had neither revolvers nor rifles; only batons. Yet they had a queer mystique, despite their absurd helmets, their boots which had become a music-hall joke. It was this mystique which intimidated the faint-hearted.

Chief Constable Wilson, clad in plus-fours and sports jacket, as though for a Sunday on the links, led his police through the opening gates. His command had an amateur informality: 'Now, boys, at

37

them.' He might have been Douglas Jardine, calling his Test team to new efforts against Ponsford and Woodful and Bradman. He carried his only weapon as Jardine carried a bat. It was an ash stick with a gnarled head and when he drew it, it seemed to be more formidable than any rifle.

In ten minutes the struggle was over. Iron doors were turned and keys turned. There were only the shouts of the defiant, the hiss of hoses fighting fires. Plymouth firemen fought the fires until the evening. Plymouth ambulance men treated about seventy casualties. Twenty of them were prison officers, four of whom were seriously injured. Twenty-three prisoners were injured by police batons, seven by rifles.

But Dartmoor families could not believe that it was over. I remember the rumours of lorries, hidden among trees to help the prisoners in a mass break-out to London and the Midlands. Every light that night was suspect. More than one moorland farmer imagined he saw lamps signalling, to and from the prison.

For several days police continued to patrol the moor. Meanwhile routine farm work, including the feeding of stock and milking of cows, was carried out by prison officers helped by students from Seale Hayne Agricultural College, Newton Abbot.

The trial of ring-leaders was held at the Duchy Hall at Princetown; normally used for political meetings and amateur concerts, for some evenings each week as a cinema. Mr Justice Finlay was appointed judge of the special Assize; and when the judge in state attended a pre-trial service at the parish church, he was accompanied by the Bishop of Plymouth at the head of other clergy and passed between lines of Girl Guides and Wolf Cubs.

The accused were between the ages of twenty-four and forty-six. Nine were found not guilty. One pleaded guilty to malicious damage from the outset and was sentenced to six months. Sixteen others were found guilty of malicious damage, while Thomas Davis was sentenced to twelve years penal servitude for 'feloniously wounding or causing grievous bodily harm to Prison Officer E. Birch.' Remissions were later granted to nearly thirty prisoners who had helped or defended prison officers.

But what one officer remembers is not the smoke and the din, not even the smouldering tension before the eruption, but the singing of a mutineer. He was a tenor. He sang 'When Irish eyes are Smiling' and a frightened town listened in amazement as his proud and beautiful voice rose from the muddle of violence and flames and rifle-shots.

Now the memory of that Sunday is part of Princetown folklore, and the singing tenor is part of it. Now prison officers pass calmly down the street; their uniforms as familiar and meaning as little as khaki in a garrison town. Violent criminals still make pets of field mice and jackdaws. Swindlers still volunteer as hospital orderlies. Men born in cities, to whom 'the countryside' used to be a park and 'keep-off-the-grass, still feed pigs and milk cows. Learned men become library orderlies; 'old lags' call themselves painters because of the building trades it is the easiest; and men guilty of sexual offences against children are still the scum of prison society.

Summer coaches bring the visitors and for a while each day the voices of Yorkshire, Wales, Scotland and London are in the town square. Some come to stare; even to fix field glasses on working parties with a calloused indifference that makes public spectacle of private humiliation. Some are ashamed. Others are saddened, feeling why Sir George McGrath, medical officer of the war prison, called it 'a great tomb of the living.' But I remember it at night. To be near it then is to hear a unique silence; as though the heart of the world has stopped.

# The Railways of Dartmoor

In the middle of the nineteenth century railroads pushed out of towns to the hills of Dartmoor. The first was the Newton Abbot to Moretonhampstead line, begun in August 1863, but not completed until 1866. It was built by the Moretonhampstead and South Devon Railways with a capital of £105,000 and was operated by the South Devon Railway. Its immediate effect was fourfold.

It dealt a death blow to the road toll, which had impeded and soured road traffic so that when the gates were at last removed, they were burned ceremonially amid cheers. It enabled working men to reach Newton Abbot, giving them a choice of employment in a busy and rapidly expanding town. It enabled farmers easily to reach the cattle and pannier markets of Newton Abbot, making smaller markets and fairs redundant. And it brought the standards of towns into the remote places. This process was begun even while the line was being built, for labourers employed in its construction received two shillings and ninepence a day. It seemed big money to the farm worker who was still receiving nine shillings a week.

The Newton Abbot-Moretonhampstead line was twelve miles long. It passed through Heathfield, Teigngrace, Bovey Tracey, Lustleigh. Its first full run was on 4th July 1866. Old women were afraid of what its sparks might do to thatch; old farmers wondered its effects on wages; employers of domestic servants deplored cheap travel, since it might persuade girls to abandon the hills of their childhood and to seek situations elsewhere. But the very young had no qualms. Boys were as fascinated by this monster as their fathers had been by the stage coach. They would have given names to the engines, borrowing those of the stage and mail coaches. But the railway companies had anticipated this need to bestow honour by establishing identity. The custom of naming engines with stage-coach names was already popular.

Railway time became the official time at Heathfield and Moretonhampstead and Lustleigh. Hitherto time had not been measured in minutes. Men had judged it by the cows at the gate or by the rooks going home. Gentlemen with sundials had checked their watches by them. Then village time became the station clock, and the porter who wound the clock realised his importance.

In those early years the station staff became a new elite, their stature not to be assessed by the number of trains nor by the degree of traffic. They had the authority of their uniforms. They had power also. They could send the eight fifteen away, leaving you a hundred yards late. Or they could say, 'Hang on a minute, Bert!' and wait for their favourites.

After the first excitement the railway had less effect on moorland life than some had predicted. Its service was inadequate. There seemed to be a grudge by remote authority against this little line. Not until its amalgamation with the Great Western Railway did the service improve with an average of six coaches in each train. In 1906 the GWR introduced connecting buses from Chagford, and by 1910 there were five trains a day each way. Morning and evening trains were packed with workers going to work and returning. But Wednesday was the peak day, when countrywomen brought their baskets to Newton Abbot pannier market. The town's development as a railway junction was bringing prosperity to Newton Abbot, and the moorland people had a small share in it.

About 1927 railway time ceased to be authoritative, for the wireless had arrived and with it Big Ben; against which no watch in any village dared to argue. But the train continued to be the only sensible way to travel; for to travel by saddle or trap was to be at the mercy of the weather, while the private car came late to Dartmoor. The peak period was the 1930s, when eleven trains a day made the run, not counting six as far as Bovey Tracey.

This is when I remember the Wednesday journey; the coaches clumsy with baskets and pushchairs, bright red with jokes and lamentations about me-feet-they's-killin'-me. Drivers knew their regulars by name. At Lustleigh they always waited for Elsie because Elsie was always late.

When they reached Newton Abbot, the people took their places at the family stalls which made the pannier market a small town.

41

They sold eggs and chicken and hogs pudding; honey and cream and carnations and cauliflowers. Not all were farmers' wives. Many had only gardens. But they managed always to find something to sell, continuing a tradition established by their grandmothers who had gathered lichen for dyes and sedge for mattresses.

Morning was their busy time at the market; punctuated by cups of tea and gossip and by more lamentations about their feet, which were now droppin'-off. In the afternoon they turned customer and bought the needs of their families at Newton Abbot shops; using their pennies shrewdly and comparing prices at Badcock's with prices at Austin's. Then to the station and to the late afternoon train; often pushing the youngest in the pushchair or carrying him on their hip in the fashion known best to countrywomen.

The journey home was always tired and slow and fretful. The driver knew better than to crack the jokes which in the morning had seemed so funny. Even Elsie had nothing to say. Quietly the train put them down at their several stations; the fireman and guard helping with the pushchair and passing out the baskets.

After the Second World War this old train continued to be busy; for petrol was rationed and private travel by road was privileged. But as peace settled down and petrol again became merely a matter of money, its character subtly changed. Those who could afford private travel had their cars. The train became a substitute. Its status was tarnished. Even the honour of being addressed by name by the driver seemed to be diminished.

Yet its end under the axe of 'economy' in 1959 was cruel and contrived. Many who had not paid a fare for years were immediately indignant. Tears were shed for the train which had borne them through two wars. Protest meetings were held. Nobody believed the assurances that a bus service would prove a worthy alternative. The indignation had a militant air. Canon O. M. Jones, of Teigngrace, led a society which was founded in protest, then confirmed in a resolve to somehow restore the line. Nobody believed that either.

The last train ran on 2nd March 1959. Recently I went back to see the bridges and viaducts so well constructed; to find the stone which made Lustleigh my favourite among stations. This stone was a memorial. It read:

42

> *Beneath this slab and stretched out flat,*
> *Lies Jumbo, once our station cat.*

There is a place in my affection for a railway station which can honour its cat in this way. But although I searched among the rambling roses that gave this station a red shine, I could not find the stone.

In cold figures the line was always a financial hazard. Its original capital of £105,000 in shares was supported by £35,000 in debentures; but the cost of building was £155,000. On 1st July 1872, the company was amalgamated with the GWR; and the process of big fish swallowing little fish reached its logical conclusion on 31st December 1947 when the GWR lost its identity within British Railways.

Teign Valley railway to Exeter was begun in 1882 but not completed until 1903. It needed twelve Acts of Parliament for its seven and three-quarter miles from Heathfield to Christow. It joined the Newton Abbot-Moretonhampstead line at Heathfield; giving that village the distinction of becoming a junction.

The Plymouth-Tavistock line was opened on 22nd June 1859. Built by the South Devon and Tavistock company it was extended northward to Lydford, then west to Launceston.

An attempt was also made to link northern towns and villages with Barnstaple in the north-west and Exeter in the east. Beginning at Coleford Junction a new line reached Okehampton in 1871.

The south-eastern villages of Dartmoor had their rail link in 1872, when the Totnes-Ashburton branch was opened on 1st May. This enabled farmers in the neighbourhood of Buckfastleigh, Buckfast, Dean Prior, Holne and Poundsgate to truck their cattle; their wives to reach Totnes pannier market each Friday with their dairy produce. In its early years its main trade was the woollen industry of Buckfastleigh, which as late as 1890 provided more traffic than Newton Abbot.

It was an early casualty in the elimination of branch lines; closed to passengers in November 1958, to goods on 10th September 1962. But a preservation society insists that it might be re-opened by volunteers.

There were changes, also, at Princetown. Sir Thomas Tyrwhitt's original iron road to Plymouth, opened in 1823, a horse-drawn tramway rather than a true railway, was dead by 1880. Part of it was reconstructed for locomotives and joined the Plymouth-Tavistock line at Yelverton. It was opened in August, 1883.

For many years the Princetown branch-line was busy, not only in trucking out granite and bringing in coal as Tyrwhitt had envisaged, but in conveying people to their favourite places on the moor. Thousands of Plymouth's swelling population had their first glimpse of Dartmoor from the windows of this train. In the years immediately before and after the First World War, when an August day on the moor was the only 'change of air' a working family was likely to get, the train was the way to holiday. But that period also passed, so that by 1955 and week-end cars and holidays-with-pay, the day-out train was an excitement which only the old understood. The branch-line was out of date and the train felt it and became small.

By 1956 it was over and those who had mocked it most and used it least were moved by sentiment to plead for it like begging money for the condemned. Only then did the post-war generation realise what their grandparents had known fifty years before; that a branch-line is never an ordinary train.

The last train to Princetown on 3rd March 1956 was garlanded and flattered. It had more friends than it ever realised. They mourned the passing of a link between Princetown and Plymouth which Sir Thomas Tyrwhitt had instigated a hundred and thirty three years before, and for which it was said that he would never be forgotten.

# Church, School and Change

In the late nineteenth century elementary education ceased to be a luxury which a prosperous nation could not afford. For the first time schools made a long arm to reach the children of remote farms and cottages. They came reluctantly. Some rode ponies, many walked long distances; unable to come in winter because of the swollen streams and splashing bogs. Those who had work to do before they left, since small farms depended on their sons, were excused attendance until ten. They became 'ten o'clock scholars.' Yet the education of country children was still considered stupid and wasteful, not only of money but of the children's time. As late as 1910 W.H.Hudson in his *A Shepherd's Life* was writing a view of rural education which was widely held in 1891.

He wrote of a boy working alone in a field: 'Better off and better employed than most of his fellows poring over miserable books in school.' In the same paragraph he sighed for a system of education 'which would not keep the children shut up in a room during the best hours of the day, when to be out of doors, seeing, hearing and doing, would fit them so much better for the life-work before them.'

The assumption is plain; that the children would find their life-work in following their fathers, remaining in the districts where they were born because that was the pattern. It did not understand what was happening in the rural schools; where not all the children were as bored as Hudson supposed them to be and where not all the books were 'miserable.' They way was being prepared for England to make an astonished and reluctant discovery; that brains and talent and ambition were not confined to any one stratum of society.

Education coincided with the improvement of roads and the development of railways. Books which the children read informed them of the world beyond the hills. The train, making smoke down the valley, showed them the way out. In the years before the First

World War the young began to take that way out; the men to trades in towns and cities, the girls to service in London or to the golden towns on the Torbay coast. Yet tradition lingered among craftsmen and farmers and others who had skills or land to pass on to their sons. The old tradition of father-to-son continued while new schools were being built and deep unrest was stirring. It was an irony that in the years when tourists first discovered Dartmoor villages and admired the survival of a way of life, those villages were becoming impatient of the restrictions and conditions inherent in that way of life.

The First World War shattered the pattern. Sons who should have become wheelwright or farrier or cordwainer in a tradition generations deep were suddenly strangers in khaki; talking of foreign places and using their new education to sign letters in mud and sand. Some did not return. Every Dartmoor community has its war memorial of granite with names in letters of slate. But more than men died in those years of hysteria and casualty lists and Old Bill. A way of life, already challenged by reformers and disturbed by education, died in the period 1914-1918.

The old of all social levels tried to retain the ways that they knew best. They looked back to the years before the war as 'the good old days;' remembering only what nostalgia selected and colouring memory with colours so false that hardship and poverty were given qualities which they did not have at the time. Tired old women, whose only means of supplementing income had been the washing of surplices or the weeding of turnips, watched in amazement, dismay or indignation as their daughters opened doors to summer tourists; finding the profit of seasonal hospitality an immediate boost to family fortunes and pioneering the 'Bed and Breakfast' sign which is now as much a part of the rural scene as the television aerial. In this way the tourists helped to bury the way of life which they were determined to admire.

Cordwainer and tailor were the first to go; for horse-drawn vans from border towns brought out cheap shoes and boots, dresses and coats of a quality so mean yet at prices so low that the village tailor could only despair. The baker continued to bake his certain shapes for certain customers. His bakehouse continued to be a warm meeting-place in winter, each Sunday morning made busy by the dinners brought to his oven by the eldest daughters of big families. But when he was old and pale, there was no son to follow. His son was in Exeter being a bank clerk, and what do you think of that? So his bakehouse closed, and a mercenary van brought bread from the border town.

The thatcher died with none to inherit his hook and biddle. Even the wheelwright could not persuade boys that there was a future as well as honour in his craft. The blacksmith looked up the hill to something new called a garage, then looked down to the hoof between his knees and plied his rasp and wondered how long. It was a sad day in a Dartmoor village when the blacksmith hung up his tallowed apron and let his forge go cold.

Each village changed as the old crafts closed, yet each retained the core of its identity because each retained its school. Through the children fragments of an old way of life were remembered like favourite photographs in a faded album. This happened at Lustleigh, where the ceremony of choosing and crowning a May Queen was cherished by those mothers who most despised the 'old days.'

The social effects of the Second World War were less than of the first. But the post-war years became a period of disturbance, stress and protest. The most significant change was the transfer of pupils over eleven from village schools to others in border towns. The purpose was admirable; making well-equipped premises available to all the children of Dartmoor and for the first time compelling them to mix with and compete among their contemporaries of towns. The side-effects were considerable.

The sense of a community was wounded. It seemed that the daily departure of senior children was a draining of village energy. Something happened to the children also. Belonging neither to a Dartmoor community nor to a town, they had loyalties to neither. They occupied an ephemeral world between village and town which seemed to be represented by the school bus. It took them a long time to become adjusted. When they did, they seemed to their bewildered parents to be more of the town than of the community where they had been born. They brought into the village a new impatience for those amenities which their contemporaries in towns already took for granted. Their standards had ceased to be village standards. They wanted change.

In the 1950s the village school, which had promised to last for ever, was diminished. Some were closed; others lived in the shadow of something called 'economy,' which became the code word of that period. The decline of the school coincided with the closing of branch-lines, which also had been built to last for ever. Each Dartmoor village changed quickly, and in nothing was this change more marked than in its church.

At one time the domination of the village church was expressed by the height of its tower. Its influence extended to the school, to youth organisations, women's guilds, charities. Its magazine was the voice of the parish. The church governed indirectly as its tower dominated symbolically.

The process of change was slow until the First World War; when men in puttees first began to question the honesty of a church which could attempt to be whatever expediency required. In the 1920s this questioning hardened to hostility; expressed in a withdrawal that isolated the church as a Sunday place and became more eloquent than criticism. Parents compromised their allegiance, despatching their children to choir or Sunday school but unwilling to commit themselves except at times of festival. The harvest festival in September became more important than Easter. Trinity and Pentecost became church words, without meaning in a world of strike and crisis and love-on-the-dole. Christmas alone survived and grew; if only as a family festival which needed carols and bells and understood its Christian significance, yet did not feel compelled to bring the church within its celebration. Hymns on the wireless became good enough.

By 1935, when I was old enough to take notice, the village church was beginning to pay for its cynicism of the eighteenth century, its social arrogance of the nineteenth. It continued to decline, despite the brave determination of individuals; the distress of those who trimmed its graves and donated its flowers; the enthusiasms of young ministers who inherited apathy, then found a harder quality behind it. This harder quality was informed by memory or by reading; and what the village remembered was not the fine sermons or the exhortations but the subtle use of power, the degradation of Christian principles, most of all the condemnation of all who did not conform.

After the Second World War the village church tried to compromise. It opened its doors to the chapel people; extended its hand in friendship even to Roman Catholics. It tried to make a virtue of weakness and to call it tolerance. It pleaded where it had commanded. The village turned away and flourished cruelly without it.

In some towers the bells still ring, but the ringers do not always attend the service which the peal proclaims. They are servants only of the bells. Choirs still sing, sustained by treble, soprano and alto, but lacking bass and tenor. Morning service is traditionally attended by those who have retired to the village; service officers and civil servants and their wives who have their favourite pews and who appear to consider that attendance is a duty. Evensong is traditionally attended by the working class. An average morning congregation is eleven. At evensong the number might be twenty. I have attended both and prefer evensong to matins; but even evensong has a dreadful pallor, with every psalm an incoherent ordeal and every hymn a joyless striving for a quality which is not there and might never have been there.

At other times the village church is important permanently as a museum of craftsmanship, occasionally as a place of baptism, of marriage and of burial. The apathy implicit in its isolation on week-days no less than in its services on Sundays finds further expression in *Venture*, copies of which are available for sixpence. This church newspaper was introduced by the Bishop of Exeter in 1962. It promised to stimulate, to bang the drum for the Christian way of life. But if this is the Christian way of life - the museum silence, the threadbare services, limp copies of *Venture* on the table - Christianity has no more relevance than the farthing; which likewise has a denomination but no value.

It is not true. I feel it must not be true. Yet the village church makes it seem true. What could have been a power for good was used as an instrument of repression in a long social struggle. This silence, this sense of mourning, is the aftermath. The village church was destroyed not by present apathy but by the cynicism and arrogance of those in places of trust within it.

## Dartmeet, the Coffin Stone and Grannie Satterley

A popular and accessible place is Dartmeet, especially favoured by weekend cars from the Torbay coast. Like Widecombe it is considered 'spoiled.' Like Widecombe it is condemned unjustly. Dartmeet celebrates the meeting of the East and West Dart, before the river tumbles down to maturity at Totnes. In the late eighteenth century it was the summer camp of gypsies.

The hill above it is Yar Tor. Its clapper bridge, built for packhorses in the thirteenth century, was ruined by floods on 4th August 1826. But few who come to Dartmeet find the Coffin Stone on the left hand side of the road tilting down from Widecombe. It is near the track which was worn by animals and people long before the road was made. It was the resting place of the dead when men carried coffins across the moor to Widecombe. They carried in relays of four or six and to carry was an honour. Women mourners followed the bearers; and at this stone they gathered to sing psalms and murmur prayers and to look up to the long climb ahead.

The custom was to carve on the stone a cross and the initials of the dead. Five crosses are discernible still. The initials among the lichen include A.C. and S.C.; A.C. for Aaron Cleave, of Hexworthy, S.C. for Samuel Caunter of Dartmeet. Others are partly obscured, but would seem to be I.B. and I.P. with two crosses. The stone is in two parts and gorse bulges out of the crack.

The coffin of Grannie Satterley was placed here in 1901, and the house which Grannie helped to build is nearly two miles from Dartmeet; up the hill towards Two Bridges, then sharp left towards the Forest Inn. Three quarters of a mile brings you to Huccaby, and on the right, beyond Huccaby Bridge, is Jolly Lane Cott. It is the last house to be built on Dartmoor in a day.

That was in Midsummer, 1832. Tom Satterley was an ostler at Two Bridges Inn. Sally was his bride. By ancient if unwritten right whoever could build a house in a day on common land was entitled to it for ever. None could evict, provided the first fire was lit by sundown. The right was cherished by the poor because it was a means towards independence; bringing with it the attendant rights of grazing on the moor in summer as well as free peat for burning and free bracken for bedding. It was resented by farmers because every new house meant more stock on the moor, and because every successful building generated unrest among other labourers.

Tom and his eighteen year-old wife chose midsummer day partly because of the long hours before sundown; chiefly because the farmers would be at Holne for the ram-roasting revels. With the help of friends, they built their house in a day, using the fund of granite stones which still litter the hillside. The walls were five feet high. The thatch sloped to meet them. There was a fireplace but no chimney. That, like the steps to the upper storey, came later; when the right was established and the work could be leisurely. The original walls remain. They can be easily seen, reaching up to the line where the second storey begins. The stream where Sally bucketed up her water is still busy. The land first turned by Tom's mattock is still tilled.

Grannie lived longer than her husband. In 1900 she sat at her door, immaculate in long black skirt, white apron and white cap. The whiteness of her apron was a matter of pride. It was to her that the Reverend Baring-Gould came when he was collecting folk songs of the moor. But Grannie would sing only as she worked, so he had to follow her to the stream and back again. She died in 1901, and Dartmoor afforded her its greatest honour. Men carried her across the heather and bracken to the church at Widecombe. Her last words were engraved on the coffin: 'Nothing in my hands I bring, simply to the cross I cling.'

# Cranmere and Duck's Pool

The source of the East Dart, West Ockment and Taw is the bogland near Cranmere, and Cranmere Pool is not a pool; only a saucer-like depression in the middle of silence. It has no attraction whatever except the challenge which its remoteness offers..

Over a hundred years ago it began to be fashionable to 'do' the tramp to Cranmere Pool and to leave a visiting card in proof of achievement. It soon became not only fashionable but a discipline.

I had the misfortune to be fifteen in the middle 1930s, when hiking was in vogue. Cranmere Pool was suggested to me as a possible motive for being alive or at least as a destination for Sunday. My cry of 'What for?' went unheeded. Young Englanders didn't put their feet on the mantelshelf and go to perdition on five Ardath and Sydney Horler. Sensible Young Englanders realised that the long trek offered challenge to that spirit which had put so much pink on the map of the world. So I was shamed into taking my feet from the mantelshelf and into pretending to be a potential Empire-builder like Harry Wharton.

Those I went with were well equipped; knapsack, spare socks, boots, stick, watch, compass. They climbed with a furious energy that appalled me; admiring the view every five minutes because that was part of the treatment, then checking by compass and assuring each other that they were not lost yet. You had to pretend to be lost somewhere on the way. That was good form. Only braggarts and spoilsports made it look easy.

I wondered if old Jim Perrott, of Chagford, knew what he was starting in 1854; when he built that little cairn in the saucer-like depression and placed in it a bottle for visitors' cards. Fifty-one years later, when untold numbers had suffered as I was suffering, Mr H. P. Hearder and Mr H. Scott Tucker came from Plymouth to donate a visitors' book. It had six hundred and nine signatures in

1905; nine hundred and sixty-two in 1906; one thousand three hundred and fifty-two in 1907 and one thousand seven hundred and forty-one in 1908. When that book was filled, the *Western Morning News* presented others, passing them on completion to Plymouth library. Subsequently Perrott's bottle grew into a granite pillar, containing a cupboard and postal box in oak. Now the act of signing in has developed into a ritual. You address postcard or letter, stamp it, frank it with a 'Cranmere' rubber stamp on the left-hand side, then leave it for the next visitor to post; playing fair by taking one from the box and posting it at a border town. Many address an empty envelope to themselves for the fun of comparing dates; the date they were at Cranmere and the date of the official franking. If the gap is several days they are pleased, since it shows how few ever reach Cranmere. It might also show how few are foolish enough to attempt it, but this sort of thinking never clouds the enthusiasm of those who like to make pilgrimages to a hole.

Anyway it didn't work for whoever wrote the letter which I took. I carefully placed it in an inner pocket, resolved to play the game; then forgot it and put the old coat away, not finding it until 6th May the following year. The poor recipient, welcoming his missive after nearly ten months, must have judged 1937 a lean year for Cranmere.

Today is different. Cranmere Pool is much less remote because the War Department has extended a road towards it from the north west. The road reaches within a mile, and there is always the chance of a friendly lift. But those who prefer the hard way can still attack it from the south and northeast. The route from Gidleigh is about six miles; from Chagford about seven.

A similar post box, if with a little more purpose, is at Duck's Pool, near the stream workings of Dark Lake. This area is similarly remote; which is why Dr J. W. Malim and other friends chose it for the erection of a bronze tablet as a memorial to William Crossing, most honoured of Dartmoor chroniclers.

Crossing was born on 14th November 1847, and died in 1928. He spent boyhood holidays in a cottage on Roborough Down; getting the 'feel' of Dartmoor in his most impressionable years. In 1872 he married Emma Witheridge, of Ivybridge. They made their home at South Brent, and Crossing's careful recording of Dartmoor

53

began. He wandered the moor and made exhaustive notes; yet he never attempted to 'do' the moor or to 'learn' it. Constant association deepened his knowledge to the point of understanding. People of all walks of life liked his modesty. They talked with him of what they remembered or of what their parents and grandparents had remembered. They contributed to his unique fund, but the more Crossing learned of the moor the less he was able to write the massive, comprehensive book which at one time he had promised.

The bronze tablet is eight and a half inches long, six and a half inches wide; set almost flush with the face of a large granite boulder. Beneath it is the letterbox; at one time a wood-lined recess, containing a zinc box about eighteen inches long and eighteen inches wide. This has been removed. In 1950 Dr Malim substituted a copper box. It contains a visitors' book, a stamp pad and a rubber stamp for 'Duck's Pool, Forest of Dartmoor.' The idea is much the same as at Cranmere Pool; you leave one postcard for the next visitor to post, then post the one which you have found.

Unhappily Crossing's friends are much less tolerant than he was. They insist that Duck's Pool is a shrine, which would have embarrassed that modest man. They also insist that 'Duck's Pool is not Hay Tor;' condemning Hay Tor for its popularity and showing that contempt for people which corrupts.

# The Committee and the Mast

Dartmoor became a National Park in 1951 under the National Parks and Access to the Countryside Act of 1949. The boundaries of the Park extend beyond the boundaries of the moor and far beyond that part of the moor which is called 'The Forest.' Because of this it includes Ashburton, the only urban area to be wholly within the Park.

A purpose of the Act was to preserve the character and integrity of those wild spaces which remain in a densely populated island. Another was to ensure that use of the Park was preserved for all people of this generation and for all those of generations to come. The implementation of those purposes was entrusted to a National Park Committee, based in Exeter and meeting once a month. Their task was difficult from the first and has been prejudiced since by the autocratic voices in which the Committee's opinions have been expressed. One voice can be heard in the official 1957 guide to Dartmoor, for which some pedant wrote of Widecombe: 'The intelligent visitor will not wish to linger in it today.' In those eleven words Dartmoor National Park Committee insults the thousands who elect to linger. On page 66 the same writer dismissed Widecombe Fair and added: 'All the roads leading to it are best avoided.' How many take heed may be judged by how many continue to take the roads to Widecombe Fair; but that such an opinion can be expressed by a Committee which needs public confidence and sympathy is an indication of the gulf between Dartmoor and Exeter.

Since 1945 there have been many changes within the boundaries of the moor. Mains electricity; washing machines; refrigerators; fast cars to gobble long distances and to make Exeter and Plymouth as accessible to Dartmoor families as Dartmoor is to the cities. The most important innovation was television.

In the middle 1950s the BBC planned to erect a television mast at North Hessary Tor; thereby bringing to moorland farms and villages, as well as to border towns, a service already taken for granted in most parts of the country. Opposition was immediate. It was bitter, articulate and organised. It was also confined almost entirely to the middle class, who used Dartmoor at weekends or who had retired in late middle age to its valleys. The substance of the opposition was that Dartmoor must be preserved; that the introduction of television would disrupt village life; and that a mast on North Hessary Tor would disfigure the skyline and be visible for long distances.

The alarm that television would seriously affect the social life of Dartmoor was out of touch. Dartmoor families hoped that the change would be immediate. They saw no novelty in remoteness. They were tired of being left out. Preservation of a skyline seemed of less importance than the introduction of London standards of entertainment, of international standards of sport.

After long controversy the mast was erected. In its refusal to be intimidated by organised opposition, the BBC did the people of Dartmoor great service. Now the mast has become a part of the tor; a thin streak on the sky which can be discerned only with difficulty and which an objecting member of the National Park Committee once could not find at all.

# Dartmoor Articles and Tales

## The Echoes of Dartmoor

I have written often about Dartmoor, and whenever I write a piece, people say: 'Very interesting, but you've left out this, that and the other.'

Of course I have left out this, that and the other; for the good reason that the full story of Dartmoor has never been told, although some day it might be. And when it is, I hope there will be a chapter on names, for the names which you hear on Dartmoor fairly dance with imagination.

There's Saddle Tor, for instance, which will remember its name when saddles are forgotten. There's Laughter Hole; suggesting that although the moor is old, it is also as young as the laughing seasons.

There's Spitchwick, which has a Dickensian ring, and Huccaby Tor, which sounds red-cheeked and rotund; and Lizwell Meet, which sounds like a tryst.

There's Bloody Pool, where death stalked the darkness and struck when eyes were frightened; and there's Great Hound Tor, where legend says that the hounds of the night come leaping.

There's Pinchaford and Cold East Cross; there's Gallant le Bower and Royal Hill. And in the sound of these names is the echo of Dartmoor; so that wherever they are heard - in Australia where no one ever queues, in New York where trains racket overhead, or in the hot silences of South Africa - they remind one of this great moor where humanity is still about six inches high and where the biggest car is still a crawling beetle.

Not even the title of National Park and the petty notices which now abound can rob this sleeping giant of its dignity.

*SDJ*

# There is a Mound with Flowers on it

The gorse is yellow, as bright as gold flying from the nugget. There's magic in the cushioned turf, youth in the old wind; and high above us is Hound Tor, perhaps the finest of Dartmoor tors, where legend says that 'wisht hounds' swooped, yowling with the gale.

Black hounds they were, with red tongues lolling; with eyes that turned the heart to dust. And near this tor, where the white road walks with dreams for company, there's a mound. A grave. And there are flowers upon it, hanging their heads for shame.

You'll find cold mention of it in *The Romance of Dartmoor* (1935) by J.W.Malim.

'It is the grave of a girl who committed suicide early in the nineteenth century, although the date is conjectural... It has a headstone and there are usually wild flowers or sprigs of evergreen placed on it, for the grave is well known to local residents.'

That's all. No answer to the questions which run around seeking answers like dogs their tails. Who was the girl; and what tragedy drove her into the arms of night? And why is this grave remembered, when so many are forgotten?

Beatrice Chase, who wrote of Dartmoor with town-bred curiosity, chanced upon it one day. She had not heard of it, but someone had; for in *The Heart of the Moor* (1914) she tells how the flowers were there 'limp and dying in the sunshine.'

She asked questions of the people round about, and learned that this was 'J's grave;' the name given by folk who could neither read nor write, and remembered names by sound alone.

Beatrice Chase tells, then, the story of a girl called Jay; an orphan apprentice from the workhouse who worked on a farm near Manaton. One day she hanged herself from a beam; for love, perhaps, for a love too secret to bear. And they buried her in a dishonoured grave beside the lonely road.

58

*The Heart of the Moor* suggests that about forty years ago, girls of the green valley came here to weep their heartbreak; and a chapter of it tells how one came here to try for death.

I am reminded now of the time I first came upon the grave; years ago it was, when the road was quiet with winter sunshine. Trees threw shadows thin and long like city spires, and all the silence stood around to watch.

I thought I was alone there, but I was not. Towards me came a man; an old man with no grumble in his walk. You got the idea that he walked slowly not because he couldn't hurry, but because the years had been good to him and because he knew that there was plenty of time.

I waited for what seemed a long time, for I'd seen the flowers in his fist.

He spoke a word with the courtesy of country places; for when strangers meet it is good to nod and put down a word, a meaningless word that does nothing to the quiet.

I did not ask questions of this man, for there was as yet no unity between us, and quick questions would have offended the answers he could give. So I watched him take away the flowers which were head-down in shame; and put on the new. Snowdrops they were, white like angels' tears and downward falling. And when he had straightened and the silence had healed between us, so that we seemed not strangers at all, I moved a hand towards the grave; a gesture which linked us. And seeing this gesture which confessed my desire to know, he began to speak; his dialect murmurous like the remembered prayers of evensong.

He told me a tale which need not be true in the way that textbooks are true, but which is true of the moor and the mystery there; part of the cottage firelight, when memory moves and sees what has never been, part of the starlight when shadows move where no shadow could possibly be.

He told me a tale of a boodiful maid, with a smile like the wild rose, and with 'air so long and dark you'd think twas night on the run. Her caught the eye of every buck in Debm, because of 'er booty dunnee knaw, but her caught the eye of the gentry too, and more's the pity, for the wan her chosed wadn never fit to buckle her shoes. Naw, nor pick up her pocket handkerchief neither. Broke 'er heart this genulmun did, everybody knawed they couldn never marry, so wan night when the wind was wild and the moon wadn no more than a rind, wan night her couldn bide it no more and comed to this yer tree and 'ere... well, 'ere her hanged herself with only the wind to make wise 'er was alive.

So moorland folk made 'er a grave and mourned 'er proper, and ever since there's always bin flowers. Even years agone, when the story wadn hardly ever told, even then there was flowers.

The old man mentioned her name only once, and that in parting. His name for her was Jane.

Perhaps the tale is true or half true, and it might be; for it belongs to the forgotten years when reapers advanced like a seeking army, and the work bullock was thrown on its side for shoeing. It belongs to the days beyond the longest memory, when the Dartmoor village lived alone, with its own thatcher and mason, preacher and blacksmith; with the tinder box for light and half-told legends for hearthside company.

And if the tale were ever true, perhaps this grave is a symbol and a reproach. A symbol of girlhood lost for ever; and a reproach to the many whose fingers reach out, long and white, to scorn the guilty heart.

Perhaps that is why this grave is remembered, why flowers atone for the cruelty done. Girlhood lies here with the rain to weep down on her, and nobody cares about the man.

*SDJ*

# The Mystery of Tom Pearce

We are being afflicted with the tale of Davy Crockett; of whom I hazard the guess that none of us had heard a word until Hollywood publicity decided that we should have opportunity to hear little else.

It is, of course, an American folktale, dressed up in song and decanted into our homes in the belief that we will welcome the familiar even when we have had enough of it. Love laughs at locksmiths. So does Davy Crockett. And the point of all this is that while the forces of entertainment, if not always entertaining, combine to make us aware of Mr Crockett, nobody pays much attention to a figure of South Devon folklore. Tom Pearce, by name. His claim to our attention the ownership of a horse, and a most remarkable generosity with it.

Between 1700 and 1850 there were many folksongs: 'The Barley Rakings,' 'Child the Hunter,' 'Strawberry Fair' and 'The Hunting of Arscott of Tetcott.' But they're remembered more by library shelves than in living song, and the only one readily recognised is 'Widecombe Fair;' to the air of which the Devonshire Regiment went marching against the Boers.

One version of this song is well-known, and it is more to gratify nostalgia than to inform that I tell the first verse:

> Tom Pearce, Tom Pearce, lend me your grey mare,
> All along, down along, out along lee,
> For I want to go to Widecombe Fair,
> With Bill Brewer, Jan Stewer, Peter Gurney, Peter Davy, Dan'l Whiddon,
> Harry Hawk, Old Uncle Tom Cobleigh and all.

It was published in 1890 by the Rev. S. Baring-Gould, who said that he had received twenty versions of it. Sometimes the tune was different, sometimes the words were altered for local allusion; but two names were common to all versions. Uncle Tom Cobleigh was never left out. Neither was Tom Pearce.

The fair varied. Sometimes it was Tavistock, sometimes Widecombe. Apparently each district had its popular destination; which shows how foolhardy it is for anyone to be dogmatic about it. A North Devon version, for instance, went to 'Hoodicote Fair,' while over the Somerset border it was 'Midsummer Fair,' and over the Cornish, 'Helston Fair.'

But the many are best illustrated by the most familiar; which shows six men riding a grey mare, while the anonymous narrator walks ahead like a man, and Uncle Tom follows behind. I've never much liked the joke implicit in this picture; and I've never much liked Widecombe's proprietary claim to the song.

I know that each year Uncle Tom is impersonated at Widecombe Fair, the grey mare too; but this custom has none save publicity value. It was begun in this century by Miss Beatrice Chase who lived at Widecombe, and who wrote popular books of enthusiasm about the village and the moor around.

But my interest is not in Uncle Tom of the many hounds and red hair. Much has been written and guessed about him. Little has been written about the man who made it possible; a quiet figure in the background whom the song calls Tom Pearce. I think him very interesting indeed, because parish records reveal nothing about him. Other names of the song are said to have come from Sticklepath, yeoman Cobleigh from Spreyton; but of Tom Pearce not a word. No place of birth. No place of death. And there might be a reason why.

There seems to me more than a frail possibility that Tom Pearce was an eighteenth century colloquialism for the devil.

There was an eighteenth century mummers' play which refers to Tom Pearce on the one hand and Our Mary on the other; symbols of evil and righteousness which remain in modern pantomimes with the Demon King on one side and the Fairy Queen on the other. In this play a man falls and dies. He is consigned to Tom Pearce, and death comes in dressed as a white-robed hobby horse. Thus Tom Pearce and his grey mare might be units of a symbol; the devil in the name, death in the horse. And the insistence on a white, or supernatural, horse supports this.

This theory is helped by two facts that link the Westcountry with South Wales; although I did not appreciate the extent of that link until reading Theo Brown in *Devon and Cornwall Notes and Queries* who says that in 1297 there was an importation of labour for the silver mine at Bere Ferrers; three hundred and eighty four miners from the Peak District, and thirty five from Wales. Mines were the property of the Crown, and skilled labour was moved frequently between the Peak District and Cornwall; which may explain the Furry Dance of Helston, an isolated example of the 'processional' type of dance which is otherwise found in one form or another in North Wales and Derbyshire.

It is possible then that the story came from Wales; first told in song or tale by the miners, and subsequently distributed and adapted until each district had its own favourite version heavily loaded with names of local significance.

If this is true the story might have begun not with the men whose names we know, but with the grey mare. Perhaps it's a variation of the Welsh custom of Mari Lwyd, when a man dresses in horse's skull and sheet; a white apparition designed to represent the skeleton of death.

So the possibility grows. What we know as 'Widecombe Fair,' a carousing song with names adjustable for topicality or local jest, becomes less a sorry joke about an over-burdened horse and more a song of death on the moor. Divorced as it should be from any one fair or locality, the tale becomes important in its symbols and superstition.

This party of men, Bill Brewer, Jan Stewer, Peter Gurney, Peter Davy, Dan'l Whiddon, Harry Hawk and the father of all Uncles, ceases to be important. They're only names, and any names will do, as other districts prove. They are names for men who are concerned more for the fair than they are for their work or land. Amusement is all they seek, and when they have no horse to take them to it, they turn to one standing by and beg: 'Tom Pearce, Tom Pearce, lend me your grey mare...'

He is, of course, the devil; although if they know it, they do not care. He produces his grey mare, strong and willing in hell's purpose; and off they go, the lazy and the irresponsible, mocking those whose backs are bowed to labour, laughing red laughs when

63

the obedient shake their heads and say: 'Tis to the devil you're riding.'

Across the moor they go; away from the sounds of men into the moorland silence. There the horse becomes the devil's skeleton, and in the rising wind they hear the devil's laugh.

It is all highly moral in the fashion of folktales. Its lesson is that to ride from work is to ride to the devil; no empty lesson in isolated communities which had to be self-supporting and could not afford idleness. I imagine that it had the approval of lords of the manor and rectors and tenant farmers, since it encouraged all to work hard lest the devil catch up with them. And I imagine that it was sung not only for the story but as a warning against the evil of sloth; just as dramatic songs used to be sung against the evils of drink.

Perhaps someone will protest that they cannot all have died on the moor; for is not Tom Cobleigh buried in Spreyton churchyard? Answers to this might be several; first that the Tom Cobleigh of the song was a name in general use for a yeoman, much as John Bull used to be a name for an Englishman. That there was a Tom Cobleigh at Spreyton, red-haired and a bachelor, cannot be doubted. He died in 1796, and was buried in Spreyton in an unmarked grave. There is a marked grave near the church of another Tom Cobleigh, who died in 1844; the son of a nephew of the older man. There is a general tendency to confuse the two, if only because seeing is believing, and that to gaze upon a marked grave is to prove the existence of the man.

Personally I doubt his importance to the song. I prefer the theory which promotes Tom Pearce from obscurity, and for this reason. It roots the song among the bones of superstition; and redeems it from the pawnshop of humbug to which commercialism has pledged it.

SDJ

# Pixie and Pitchfork

I do not remember when I first came to Dartmoor. Putting memory to the test and straining it to its fingertips, I remember the lamps of a trap; warm thumbprints of light that made the darkness smile.

Memory tells me of the silver sounds of homeward hooves; and I see the rhythmic quarters of the mare, the colour of tea which has no milk in it. I see the intelligence of her ears; hear her stumble once and snort, reproaching herself, for she is the eyes of the trap and all that we come upon she sees first.

I hear my grandfather going 'Kip, kip,' more to console the quiet than to encourage the mare; and because I am eight years old and boys of eight know these things, I know that such sounds offend the mare. For she needs no telling that she is going home.

My grandfather smelled of serge and the leather of leggings; but at that time I attributed to him the smell which the family Bible had. He was religious and fierce with it; which made life very difficult for those who had to live with him. And when I remember the trotting lamps and the silver hooves and the moor hunched star-wards like a sleeping shoulder, I imagine that he had a Bible in his pocket. Although I suppose he had not.

To remember him and his proud white beard, so white you'd think winter had got into it, is to remember the ferocity of his religion; and simultaneously to distrust those who write about the superstitions of the moorman in an uneducated age.

You hear credulous stories about pixies. You hear about the great black hound which moved like the darkest shadow of night. You hear about the body from Tavistock on moonlit pilgrimage; and the plight of men, dead these centuries, who trusted the moor and were betrayed, and who are still seeking their way home. If you know Widecombe well, you might be persuaded that pixies and whimsy are good investments; but the more I read of them, the more do I believe that such stories have been born not out of moorland ignorance, but out of educated fancies.

Scholars have found themselves alone on the moor of a night, and have been terrified by what the moorman knows to be true. That darkness does not destroy. That life goes on, so that Dartmoor moves with life where the startled eye cannot see. Such an experience has sparked the fancies of men of town and city; and these fancies, born of fright or surprise, have been remembered afterwards in library pens.

I imagine one, fat with such lore, asking of my grandfather: 'Do you believe in pixies?' And I imagine that the nearest tor would have needed to hold its hat; for my grandfather would have shouted, and when he shouted the hills winced like so many fat-heads on the morning after.

He would have answered such a tomfool question with either a pitchfork or truth; and the truth is he had one belief, and that so tremendous it trampled all others to the smithereens of nonsense.

He believed Up There and Down There; and when he mentioned either, his finger pointed so that a boy's eyes tried to see beyond the smoke of clouds, then beyond the sour peat.

He believed not in God but in Jehovah, and when he spoke of Jehovah, there was thunder of threat in the name. His Jehovah was mighty and vigilant, noting all the sin of the world and preparing to punish it with rising wind or falling prices, with storm or sickness or the lightning-stroke of death.

My mother, of another, meeker generation, spoke mildly to me of a God of love; so different from my grandfather's Jehovah that I did not confuse them. I had no doubt that when I did something I shouldn't, grandfather's Jehovah wouldn't be deceived; and that when the night was filled with wind, my mother's God was watching, promising not to blow the candle out.

Jehovah was so linked in my mind with grandfather, that when he went to market, Jehovah went with him; and the granite farm in the side of the hill was quiet, with the new milk of women's laughter spilling in it. I learned to suppose that market day was God's day. The other days of the week were Jehovah's; when the boy who left a gate open knew what was coming to him.

That is my memory of the moorman who lived his youth by tinder box, and who detected the hand of the devil in paraffin since paraffin was strange enough to be new. He and his kind believed not in pixies or in any other decorative whimsy, but in a great and muscular Jehovah at perpetual war with sin.

I remember my grandfather the night the cow was sick. He came into the kitchen, lantern in hand, and when he looked around, everyone knew that the cow had died and that such a death was a Judgment. For that was the question in his stare. Which one of you has sinned? Which has brought the Judgment on us? And I remember how my grandmother took the lantern from him and put it out. And how the daughters looked down at their darning. And the sons bent forward, eyes on their boots. And I remember how guilt sat in the silence, as real as a cat, and how the kitchen waited for the vengeance of Jehovah to be echoed in the vengeance of the father.

I've heard it pretended that the moorland farmer was afraid of darkness, when the spirits were moving to plot against him. This is absurd; for in winter half the working day was darkness, and the working day was such that there was no time in it for fears. Servants from the rectory might run wide-eyed past the tree where once a gypsy had swayed in the night wind; but servants from the rectory were silly creatures to all save those who wished to marry them. And none believed that kitchen maid Sarah had been chased by anyone, least of all by a ghost who had all the world to choose from.

Tellable stories, discredited at the time, have been credited since by those who have wished to invest the moor with something marketable called 'atmosphere.' If you'd shown whimsy to my grandfather he would have put a boot on it. And if ever he had met a pixie, he would have quoted Elijah and that would have been that.

In other ages, even more than today, families of the moor were concerned with getting a livelihood out of it. And when so much had to be done for so little, there was no time for pretty fancies.

And yet memory, though I coax it, will not go back to the beginning. I cannot remember when first I came to Dartmoor. A part of my childhood grew there, so that I looked around without surprise, and knowing no contrast, learned to take it all for granted. This was my loss, and now looking back, I wish that I could have come new to it when the dins of other places were stale in my ears.

If I were going there for the first time, I would go in the evening when the world is closing over like the wild flower. I would go where the valleys are treed with silence, and there I would listen. And if I listened carefully, so that all the moor became as silent as a church, I would hear the crying of the twilight waters. The heart swells to that sound, so melancholy is it, and elusive; and I count it my loss that I cannot remember when first I heard it or when the hearing of it was breathless with surprise. Such moments in life are rare, and should have a place in memory. Not to remember them is to lose what cannot be repeated.

*SDJ*

# How Dartmoor Beat Big Business

This is the season when families, coming in from the whiplash of rain and the bruising cold, turn with gratitude to their fires.

The great log fire, talking with many tongues, is in the best Devon tradition; but the fire of the Dartmoor labourer was of peat. A merry fire, too; especially when it was carefully built in 'yaffuls' upon the eagerness of furze.

To cut as much peat as he needs has long been one of the privileges of the Dartmoor commoner. He has used it exclusively for burning; but at one time men saw in peat the promise of wealth.

Princetown became the centre of this attempt at turning peat to gold. Its prison was opened for French prisoners of war in 1809. War ended in 1815 and the prisoners went home; branded for ever by their memories of this cold, damp forest of stone where water dripped like the blood of the dying, and where the sounds of men were mocked in the devil's echo.

By 1818 Princetown was a funeral town; and men, standing on the hill to look down on it, shivered in their souls. But not Sir Thomas Tyrwhitt.

He looked down on Princetown and saw not the ghost of misery moving, but a granite settlement which could become a prosperous town. He planned a campaign against the skinflint moor; to demand goodness and charity from it in the growing of grain and flax and hemp. Above all he planned to export peat to towns; since coal was expensive and mining dangerous, and since the case for a new household fuel seemed plausible.

His schemes were fine, and included the building of a railway; but they came to little. Peat burns dirtily, leaving a grave of ash, and it was not popular in towns. Moreover, the growing of grain and flax and hemp cost more than it could ever return.

For years Princetown became the dead town of the moor; but in 1844 three men, of whom Mr Peter Adams of Plymouth was one, saw the possibilities of extracting oils and naphtha from the peat. The prison became a factory; with a railroad linking it to Omen Beam and Greena Ball, where beds of peat were fat. Labourers were employed to cut it at so much a 'journey.' This 'journey' was an agreed stint of forty yards in length, and twice the width of the spade. Cutting was heavy, skilful work, and the labourer who could cut two 'journeys' a day earned high pay.

The oils and naphtha venture cost £19,000, but it didn't succeed. After a few years the prison was silent, not to be occupied again until it became a convict prison in 1850.

Even then peat continued to be used for fuel and the making of gas. Little coal could be brought to the prison, as this was before the opening of the Princetown-Tavistock railway, so the convicts cut peat for fuel and the manufacture of gas for lighting.

Peat was in the news again in the late nineteenth century, when the West of England Peat Company worked the beds at the head of Rattle Brook. Much money was spent. A railway linked the peat-beds with Bridestow. But soon the combined difficulties of transport, Dartmoor weather and finding adequate markets were too much for the company.

It gave up, and the moorland winds screamed their delight; for there's an old verse to illustrate how jealously Dartmoor defends itself against the exploiting plan:

> *Vur when the gentlemen come out, old Dartymoor to 'tack,*
> *They vind they often got to pay fer scratchin' of his back.*

The suggestion is that Dartmoor is hostile to commerce; resenting the invasion of an army of machines and men. The suggestion is, too, that the moor has a being which can be offended, a patience which can be shrewd. It allows the businessman to come; shows him enough to tempt him, then waits until railroads have been built and gold has been buried in the excitement of endeavour. Then it breaks that endeavour in the silence of snow and the scream of winds; defending itself with all the resources of a wilderness affronted.

Only the quarrying of its granite has proved over many years a profitable business. But Dartmoor was discerning in its resistance. It allowed small men to scratch its surface and to make a profit out of the sale of peat in a small way. It allowed the humble workman to succeed where big business failed, and late in the nineteenth century peat was still taken by packhorse and donkey to nearby market towns.

Ashburton was one of the towns. Its streets remember the plod of packhorses down the long hill from the moor. The poor who could not afford coal used to come to the market where the horses stood; there to buy peat at so much a 'lot.' Big 'lots' at a shilling each to the fairly rich. Small 'lots' at a penny for the poor. Peat was used by women who took in washing for a living; but the housewife who could afford coal scorned it, not because it was niggardly of heat but because of the litter of ash which filled the grate. This ash is called 'briss' [in the 'Portrait of Dartmoor' it is the variant 'bistle'] and makes the polishing housewife furious.

Now commerce has forgotten its schemes to tame the moor. Women and children no longer collect lichens from the granite near Okehampton, to be sent to Plymouth and exported for the making of dyes (Sedge was gathered and sent to Plymouth, too, for the making of mattresses).

Grand schemes have been tried and Dartmoor has broken them. Now it is content to sleep. A National Park with many of its furies spent. And with a National Park Committee to defend it against any change at all.

*SDJ*

# Parliament that was Destroyed

Now is the time to go to Dartmoor; when the blood of summer corrodes the bracken, spilled there and left to rust, like a warning for young spring.

This is the time of colours; when the bracken has sometimes the domestic glow of cinnamon, and when the gorse flowers are the gold of remembered sunshine. Even the grass changes; sometimes soft and secretive, like the hollow of a throat, sometimes yellow, like life left too long in a forgotten cupboard.

It is the time when Dartmoor has many moods. Mist drifts like the smoke of graveyards, with trees walking out of it like men. Rain seeps, never of the sky and seeming never to reach the ground; but shivering half way. It is because of this rain, so numb with cold, that young fingers are swollen and red. Hail, like wedding rice, lies in forgotten pockets. And sometimes the wind strikes with the shriek of teeth in wood.

Lapwings, black and white, give their wings to it and drift. Ponies seem smaller than ever; wet and ragged, scavenging a living. Only the sheep pretend indifference. They stand in heather as burned as breakfast toast; and because their legs are thin and black, it seems that they wear the long stockings which housemaids used to wear in the days of sovereigns.

This is what you see when you stand and stagger and catch your breath and stand again on High Willhays, two thousand and thirty nine feet, and the highest point in England south of Cumberland. But it is not the highest tor.

Some confuse the hills and tors of Dartmoor. To be a tor a hill must have granite upon it, and some of these rock piles are famous for their shapes. Bowerman's Nose near Manaton is one; seamed and cracked and broken by rain to something like a human profile. Vixen Tor, near Merrivale Bridge, is another; sometimes called the

'Sphinx' because it resembles mildly the snub-nosed guardian of the desert.

Saddle Tor, near Ilsington, is the shape of a heavy hunting saddle; while Gidleigh Tor is called Princep's Folly because Mr Princep began to build a house there before the wind changed his mind. Best known, of course, is Hay Tor, spelt 'Hey' less than fifty years ago. It is one thousand four hundred and ninety feet high, but so accessible that almost it is tamed, worn small by familiarity which can change all things.

A favourite is Great Mis Tor, which has a rock basin on it. Folklore calls this the Devil's Frying Pan, and the story is that one night the devil, wearying of life below, came up to view the world which blames him for so much. He found his vigil cold, and beguiled the thin, mean hours by frying himself a meal. Eggs and bacon, perhaps.

This is the sort of story which belongs not to the horned purveyor of evil, but to 'Old Nick,' a much less serious and formidable figure; the sort of devil who might have a sense of humour. You change a character by changing its name, as every playwright knows.

There's a story about Belstone Tor, one thousand five hundred and sixty eight feet, with its head in the clouds some days. Once a wall was built on the west side of it, near the borders of Okehampton common. It was called the 'Irishman's Wall,' believed to have been built by an Irishman to enclose the commons from the Forest of Dartmoor. Enclosure of any kind was a reprehensible business, especially by a 'foreigner,' so the men of Belstone and Okehampton marched against the wall like an avenging army and overthrew it. The Belstone story is that the Irishman took the hint, so that his stones died where they fell. His wall never came to life again.

There's Bea Tor, where in 1887 the artist William Widgery erected a granite cross to mark Queen Victoria's Jubilee; and there's Yes Tor, at two thousand and twenty nine feet the highest of the tors, but not the most important.

Historically the most important is Crockern Tor, where miners held their Stannary courts, a sort of 'Parliament on the Hill' to discuss the business of mining in Devon.

Early in the seventeenth century there were tables and seats of moorstone on Crockern Tor, and the hill continued to be used for parley until 1749. Then, late in the eighteenth century, the parliament was destroyed; apparently by the owner of Prince Hall, who fancied the stones for other purposes. Some were taken to Prince Hall; at least one was taken to a farm where it became part of a water trough, and very successful, too.

Whatever the individual fate of the stones, it is certain that the tables and seats of the 'open' parliament were destroyed at that time. A sad story. Some may get up to protest: 'What a shame;' which it was. And: 'What vandalism.' Which it wasn't.

Two hundred years ago, and less, Dartmoor belonged to the people who lived on it. They saw stones lying around, doin' nort, no good to nobody, bin there ever since me granfer's day; and when they needed a new gatepost, they chose one for size and hauled it from wherever it had been to serve a mundane but essential purpose. Theirs was not the destruction of indifference; simply the common sense of seeing what could be used and using it.

They were crude times, with improvisation not a cleverness but a necessity. Materials for building and repairs had to come from round-about, for wheeled vehicles came late to Dartmoor, and transport of any kind was either impossible or impracticable, or at any rate expensive. So the moorman saw nothing reprehensible in adapting to his needs those materials which he could get for nothing.

He could not read and he could not write; and had he been able, he would not have read about menhirs and alignments. History began with his grandfather's fireside stories and memories. If he had a wall that needed small flat stones, he remembered a pile which he had seen since boyhood, and decided they'd been idle long enough. "Us can make use of they,' he said, and did. Perhaps the wind screamed 'Kistvaen!' but if it did, he refused to believe that his litter of stones could be a sepulchural chamber which libraries would record with relish.

I know men and women, and so do you, who stalk the moor like a squire his acres. They have a sense of ownership and of pride, which is good. And they wish to keep it to themselves, which is bad. They talk of coach parties with a sneer; of family cars and weekend trippers too. They resent the many, and that's a cold thing on any excuse.

I've met and heard the bigot, who not only resents coaches and cars, the family picnic and the army exercise, but who dismisses impatiently those who have lived for generations on the moor and whose livelihoods are deep on it. I've heard him say, as perhaps you have, for there are many of him, 'These people are ruining Dartmoor. It should be stopped. It's vandalism.'

So we're back to that word again, and the intolerance which is implicit in it.

The farmer who took granite for building wasn't a plunderer or anything as cloak-and-dagger. Rather he was a workman trying to build a life on the moor with the materials readiest to hand.

That's something which those who chatter most about Dartmoor, its kistvaens, menhirs, barrows and alignments, have never tried to do.

*SDJ*

# The Storm and the Forest

The month was October; when the moor was rusted like life on the shine of a blade.

The day was Sunday; and by horse and foot the people came to Widecombe. To this church they'd come since 1260; for Lydford church was the only church in the Forest of Dartmoor and Lydford was far away.

Most of the ancient tenements were in the south-east part of the Forest, so it was the custom for tenement holders to make their offerings at Widecombe and to pay 'Widecombe-in-the-Dartmoors' a tithe of lambs. All other tithes went to the vicar of Lydford.

They were assembled there on this Sunday in 1638; kneeling while the sky went still and became bloated with the threat of storm.

The storm grew, darkening the moor like a judgment. It exploded upon Widecombe church; each lightning flash as livid as truth. And afterwards, while the frightened scars still burned, thunder came in, a dry crackle then a blundering, forcing men and women to smallness.

Lightning attacked the church. Stones fell from the tower with a tumult of their own. The church waited like the doomed, and in the sudden stillness a voice spoke for the fearful, asking should they not seek safety outside. Somewhere. Anywhere.

Calmly the Rev. George Lyde replied: 'It is best to make an end with prayer, for it were better to die here than in another place.'

But the church did not die. The storm relaxed; lightning became pale and thunder a mumble. Widecombe lifted its head; stood up; then went slowly out to a moor that smouldered like an animal which remembers.

The storm of 1638 is still talked about in guides and reference books; perhaps because it attacked the church which generations have called the Cathedral of the Moor.

Said to have been built by tin-miners as a thanks offering, its granite tower has a sharpness of detail that thickens other towers to clumsiness.

To come upon that tower, when evening reflects itself like wine in a silver spoon, is to be proud of the men who built it.

Only in one other part of green England have I felt the same detachment, the same sense of isolation without loneliness. And that was one evening at Oxford, when spires against the sunset were of the stuff that dreams are made of.

Early in the eighteenth century Dartmoor was said to be 'richer in its bowels than in the face thereby.' This was true, for attempts to enclose the moor and to grow grain were expensive failures.

Those who lived beyond the moor, and whose caution has not been conditioned by it, have always been free with advice for those who live within it. And at the end of the eighteenth century, when Dartmoor began to attract more attention than it had received since King John, advice was frequent that the moor could be tamed and profitably cultivated.

The Dartmoor farmer, wise in the experience of generations, left experiment to the new, and continued to use the moor for the free pasturing of sheep and cattle. What grain he grew was for his own bread-making. Probably it was rye; for rye-straw was used for thatch. Late in the nineteenth century, the power layer of thatch in old buildings was usually of rye-straw.

But there was enough cultivation to warrant the building of a mill in the Forest. First mentioned in 1303, it was built by the king's tenants at their own cost. Three hundred years later it was still being used by freeholder of the Forest.

This brings the question: what is the Forest of Dartmoor?

Its boundaries were established in 1240, and re-established in 1609 when Okehampton was the scene of a Court of Survey.

Jurors were Edward Skirrett, Walter Hele, Roger Cole, Henrie Burges, Richard Edmond, Gregory Gaye, John Bickford, Hugh Ulford, John Masye, Roger Drake, Walter Lillicrappe, John Chubb, Stephen Taverner, Andrew Haywood, Roger Wickett, William Searall, Robert Hannaford, John Willes, John Hele, Walter Tookerman, William Mudge, William Ibert, Thomas Turges, Ellies Harryes and John Parnell.

Take a look at these good names and true; then recognise how many have survived as honest names do. They are green with life still, although the spelling of some has changed.

The court sat before Sir William Strode, and auditor of the Duchy of Cornwall, Richard Connocke.

'The said jurors upon good testymonie showed them, witnesses sworne and uppon their own knowledges do p'sent upon the'r oaths as followeth… the bounds of the fforest of Darmoore.'

By 1900 the old boundaries had been mildly altered and always inwards; so that the venville or common lands were widened and the Forest diminished. But for the most part the boundaries, first declared over seven hundred years ago by twelve knights, summoned to conclave by the Sheriff of Devon, have remained.

Fifty odd years ago they were declared to be from Chapel End, on the East Ockment, to Belstone Tors, Cosdon, Hound Tor, Stone Tor, Woodlake Head, across the Little Teign to King-de-Stone, King's Oven, and on by Wallabrook to the East Dart.

Thence to Dartmeet by the West Dart to Drylake Foot, Corfield Ford, Knattleborough, Western Wellabrook, Huntingdon Cross, Eastern Whitteburrow, Plym Head, Eylesburrow, South Hisworthy Tor, Princetown, Mis Tor to Deadlake Head to Rattlebrook and Sourton Tor, Langaford, High Willes, Rough Tor to Halstock Manor and back to Chapel End.

The area is more than fifty thousand acres, and is within the parish of Lydford. It has belonged to the Duchy of Cornwall since the Black Prince, and was first owned by Richard, Earl of Cornwall, under a grant from his brother Henry III.

The term 'Forest' might perplex some. It has been defined as 'an area within which wild animals and birds were protected for the pleasure of the King.'

Around it are the commons, forming parts of twenty-two border parishes. These venville parishes, in a belt of moorland around the Forest, used to be called the Commons of Devonshire. Parts of thirty-four parishes contribute to the whole of Dartmoor, but the Forest is entirely within one. It's as well to know and appreciate these things about our lovely and much-abused Dartmoor. To know them is to understand that when you walk the moor you are walking where dim centuries have trod.     *SDJ*

# Swayling – an Honoured Custom

Fires were burning in the dark. They prowled across the moor, gobbling the bracken and faking red wounds on the underside of clouds. This is the time for swayling; when hill farmers burn back old bracken, letting sunlight come to the dark earth and fortifying new growth with the ashes of the old.

It is an honoured custom. I remember hill farmers cutting wide gullies to box in the flames. They used long-handled spades and worked with an easy rhythm, never stooping or seeming to hurry. Boys carried wet sacks to control the spread, for controlling the fires was important. You did not burn the same hillside too often.

It was years before I realised that townspeople considered swayling to be a red spree, a sort of glorified bonfire night, which endowed anyone with a right to burn. This fallacy persists. There are cars which come to Dartmoor in February and March for the purpose of watching the burning and being excited by it. I suspect that when they find no fires, they yield to the fascination of the primitive and start their own.

Swayling is criticised by naturalists because it destroys life in the bracken and heather. Hill farmers retort that birds nest late on Dartmoor and that responsible swayling is finished before birds make their settling places. Specious arguments can be made for or against. Those know best about the moor who have never had to drag a living from it.

For me it is part of the long ago, when Dartmoor people lived in a world within the horizon. They were shut in by the weather. They lived with the wind and rain. They knew every fold of the land they could see, but only when they brought wool by pack-pony to the mills of towns did they venture across the granite skyline. Then they became foreigners. Even their language was different, so harsh that the people of Ashburton and Chagford could not understand it.

Swayling was the February custom. After that came the lambing, always late on Dartmoor compared with valley flocks, and always important because Dartmoor has always been sheep country. In

April and May came the foaling. There have been 'wild horses' in the neighbourhood of Ashburton for at least eight hundred years, and the pony crop is only slightly less important than sheep to the hill-farmer. Foals cost nothing. They represent all profit. Prices were high when ponies small and strong were needed for the mines. When that market collapsed, another developed, and mongrel ponies now fetch high prices as first-rides for children.

Peat was cut in the early summer. It was cut from peat-beds, several feet down, with a double-purpose tool. One edge was for cutting. The other was a spike for spearing and throwing. The pieces were thrown on one side, seven pieces wide. Dartmoor liked that number. It was supposed to be endowed with special qualities. Seven steps in a stone staircase. Seven stepping-stones. Seven children. The peat-cutter's seven pieces asked for luck from the weather.

A dry summer dried the peat and prepared it for winter burning. In the autumn it was brought down by pony. It gave a slow heat, and fires made from it were half dead with ash.

Peat is derided now. But to the Dartmoor families it was as important as water. It provided one of the first essentials during a Dartmoor winter. It provided warmth. Only those who have suffered months of crippling cold know the wonderful mercy of warmth. When the moor was paralysed by snow, the fire became more important than food. The old huddled near it. The young were saved by it. Whole families slept near it, so that the smell was in their clothes, even in their hair.

It wasn't long ago that Dartmoor was a granite wilderness with its own people and legends and customs. That past seemed nearer as I smelled the smoke and heard the crackle and watched the sky turn colour. The silent figures of a hundred years ago seemed to be in the red light. Tall men and shawled women, with pain deep in their faces and poverty in their bones. They were not there. Yet they seemed to be there. They had the moor to themselves and the wavering flames.

*MDA*

# House in a Day

A crack of light appeared in the eye of Dartmoor. The light had green in it, promising the sun. Along the moorland tracks tall shadows came; labourers all and silent, their meeting place a muddle of granite and reed.

It might have been the graveyard of a house, but it was not. It was the place where, before nightfall, a house would be.

William Skillett stood in the growing light; watching the shadows as they came and counting them, for numbers were important. The more who helped, the quicker the house would be built; for in this year of 1800 it was the law of Dartmoor that if you built a house and enclosed land between sunrise and sunset, that house, that land was yours. Yours for ever.

Skillett counted the shadows and excitement grew in him, so that he clenched his fists and shivered his shoulders. Seven friends came out of the darkness. Seven would be enough.

He glanced a smile at his wife. Yesterday they were married. Today they would have a home. His smile was sure of that now, for these friends were strong, willing to work until the sweat ran down. He went forward to greet his friends.

They spoke in whispers, aware of the conspiracy. They knew that if they were discovered, tenement farmers would ride down the work; for new enclosures were bitterly opposed.

The light in the east grew stronger. They fell to work in a silence grim and determined.

The house was of two storeys and the walls were built of granite stones, roughly squared. The door was low but wide enough for cattle, since the lower storey was divided. Man and wife on one side. Their cattle on the other.

They made steps to the upper storey and these steps were wall-stones of rough shapes. Soon use would polish them like old pennies and long polishing would wear them biscuit thin.

The upper storey was divided, too; a loft for hay, the rest for a bedroom. The loft was more important than the bedroom. Cattle would be fed from there when winter snow leaned against the door.

By the end of the day a house was up. The men stood back and wrested the salt of sweat from their mouths. They had a moment of deep, tired happiness.

Then Skillett stiffened. Towards them rode a tenement farmer, and like a dog prepared for aggression, Skillett went to meet him. Now he had something to defend.

The farmer reined his blowing horse. He looked at the house. He looked down at Skillett. The men drew nearer, saying, 'Fair do, maister, he beat the sun and you know the law.'

It was no law; no written law. It was a law made and understood by generations, and custom is formidable. They knew that tomorrow the farmer would defend the cottage and the right to build it; not because he cared about Skillett, but because he was quick to defend all rights.

The farmer rode away. He would protest about it among other tenement farmers; but he would do nothing, realising that to defend all rights, even when they were abused, was more important than the pulling down of a poor man's cottage.

Skillett went into his house, where the first fire gave it a heart. Peat smoke crawled and above it went the pot on its hook; where it would stay while years grew old in the faces of the young and Dartmoor yielded what it must to the seeking plough.

William Skillett made a plough of wood and called it his 'sull.' With it he tamed his patch of soil, and the grain which he grew was threshed with a flail. He called it his 'dreshel.'

On his one horse he depended like a blind man on his stick. It was used for all work; as a packhorse mostly. Curved poles called crooks or 'crubs' were used to keep loads in the pack-saddle; and the regular burdens were furze for kindling, peat for fuel, ferns to bed his cattle. All were cut from the moor, for he was a 'Commoner' now and had his moorland rights.

He wore a long loose tunic of flannel. It came down to his knees, and beneath it were breeches with the knees thickly patched. He wore leggings called 'skiddybats,' and his boots were huge; made by the cordwainer with iron plates added by the blacksmith. These were called 'tackling.'

He built stone walls to face the wild winds. He used the mattock like a weapon of aggression. He worked from dawn to dark and his wife worked with him; her skirt tucked up, her arms as strong as green wood. In 1830 he built a chimney for his house.

William Skillett died at the age of forty seven; a man of bearded silence, bowed by work but fierce with pride. The tenancy of his farm passed to his son. The son built a new house in 1846. But his mother would not live there.

She stayed in the house which had been built in a day. She stayed there until the end; and the end was a morning when the birds were singing. She sat beside the fire and slept and the sleep became death; and that was the end of mother's house. The house which father had built.

None lived there again. It was left to the wind, and the long white winds of Dartmoor destroyed it.

*GC*

# The Memories of Dolly Trebble

She lived in a cottage above Dartmeet. Her name was Dolly Trebble.

She lived with the wild winds and the moonlight; a little old woman shrivelled and bowed, with long memory in her eyes and the paths of friends to her door.

Her memory reached back to the noble lord of Tor Royal; to the gifts and the blandishments, the promises of wealth. She remembered her brother who was rich with wax. And with a smile in the middle of memory, she remembered Tom, tall and lean and weather-burned, who had taken her to Lydford that she might be his for ever.

The story began long ago, when Dolly lived near Princetown with her young and earnest brother. She knew she was beautiful, and liked it. She knew she was admired, and liked that, too. Yet when the quality reached out and thought she was theirs, she laughed and escaped, and led them all a merry dance.

But there was one who would not be led a merry dance. He was a moorman, Tom by name, whose silences were long and fierce, who saw evil in the laughter and disaster in the future. She scorned him and mocked him; and Tom remained, watching from a distance, watching from the moor.

Disaster moved a stride nearer when the noble lord of Tor Royal refused to let Dolly laugh and escape. He reached out for her, and went on reaching when Dolly's laughter said she was not to be had. He courted her and flattered her, and when he pressed fine gifts, her brother seized them in jealous rage and shattered them and turned to face the noble lord; defending his sister who was all he had, and shouting his mistrust in a silence hot as fire.

But even a brother can have his price, and this brown lad could not resist when the noble lord offered him a life beyond the line where the moor and sky cried quits.

He went by coach to London; given an appointment in the House of Lords. His task was the lighting of candles; his privilege the keeping of the ends of wax tapers. These could be sold for money; big money to one whose pockets had always been poor.

So the brother said good-bye, and Dolly knew as she watched him go, that a part of her life was dying; that the young, confiding days were done and that they'd never meet again. Then she raised her head to the excitement of the present; to the news that the Prince had come.

The Prince Regent paid an informal visit to his bleak waste called the Forest of Dartmoor. If he came to see a forest without trees, he stayed to see Dolly; whose beauty was such that winter ran away from her.

Day after day the Prince paid calls, and the noble lord was honoured that his favourite should have royal favour. But Tom Trebble broke his long and smouldering silence, and came riding out of the moor to pluck Dolly into his arms and onto his pony; and when his stout little pony reached the shelter of a hill, he set her down. Then he got down too, putting his hands on her shoulders and speaking to her eyes. 'I'm taking you to Lydford,' he said, 'where I shall marry you and keep you safe.'

They were married there without delay or complaint, and came back to a lonely cottage above the waters of Dartmeet. Only Tom knew the way, for there was no path to guide; and the pony stumbled among boulders and blew tiredly at the twilight, and when they reached the cottage, Tom showed her the moor with a sweep of his arm and said, 'There's your kingdom; all you can see is yours.'

There they lived for many years; Tom going about his work with cattle and sheep, calling to her when he was still far off so that she'd come to the door and wave and wait, and let him see the sunlight in her hair. They were busy there and happy; and when Tom died, suddenly, like a lie which you want to deny and cannot, she grew old and lonely, and the light of merriment went out.

She found work at the tin-mine of Hexworthy. Men admired her quiet endeavour, and though the work was hard, they made it lighter; saying among themselves, 'There goes a fine old woman, there goes a lady.'

Life closed for her gently, like the flower of night. She grew too weak for work, her eyes too dim and her feet too foolish; so the miners sent gifts, and their wives came often, making long paths where no path had been.

In those fading days, when tired memory played erratically with time, she spoke often of the past, of herself as young as morning, with her hair down her back long and golden like the longest days of summer. She spoke of the brother in London; was he rich now, with carriage and horses bought from taper ends? And she spoke of Tom who'd been young and jealous, it was funny to remember.

She talked often with half a laugh in her talk, and the women of the moor said 'yes, yes,' and didn't understand; for how could they know about those far-off days when even the Prince, the Prince Regent... fancy that now! How long ago it seemed.

She fell asleep remembering, and the curlew cried its mourning cry and the waters of the Dart were a hymn in memory. Men from the mines carried her towards Widecombe, seven miles away; and the women followed, dressed in white skirts with white kerchiefs pinned cross-wise to cover their shoulders. They moved slowly across the granite silences of the moor. They gave their voice to the wind, and the words in the wind were a psalm.

'He maketh me to lie down in green pastures...'

They took her to Widecombe and a sheltered grave, and her house was left to the starlight. There she'd been young and happy; had thrown her laugh to the morning and bade the lark be glad. There her feet had worn stones smooth; her sleep had grown used to the moonlight. There she had lived and learned to be old. Now she had no need of it; for the last of the psalm was remembered in the wind.

'And I will dwell in the house of the Lord for ever.'

*SDJ*

# Wise Woman of the Moor

Her name was Lucy. She was a kitchen maid at the rectory; and as she slipped from kitchen light to the treed-in darkness of the servants' path, her manner was startled and mildly furtive. A girl on a secret journey.

She wore her Sunday coat; her Sunday hat securely pinned. They were to give her confidence. She wore cotton gloves, too, watered mauve in colour; and they were to conceal.

Lucy wore gloves at every opportunity. When she had to take them off, her eyes were hot and heavy and melting, and when someone noticed her hands and looked up in surprise, she bit her lip in shame.

She had gone to the doctor for help. He'd prescribed this and that, and in the candle-lit privacy of her room, Lucy had followed instructions with a fervour religious. But to no purpose. She was sure about that; and when she dared tell the doctor that her hands were worse, he admitted the possibility in a grimace and counselled patience. They would go as suddenly as they had come, if only she'd be sensible and patient and stop worrying about what couldn't be helped.

But you can't be sensible and patient when you're young and ashamed. And because her shame walked with her like a shadow, she hurried through the evening village towards the cottage where the candle burned.

Lucy knocked, and after a while the candle moved, flying like a wing of light so that the window died. The door opened and Lucy looked at the candle, then at the Wise Woman behind it. She was frightened but she did not run away.

The door opened wider and Lucy went down two steps to the stone-flagged kitchen. It was a kitchen with a dresser and table, three chairs and a cat; no different from all the other kitchens of the village, and this surprised Lucy, who had made a witch of the Wise

87

Woman and had supposed her kitchen to be a private world of spells.

The Wise Woman poured strong tea from the pot that stewed on the hob. She pushed a cup towards Lucy, sitting opposite so that the candle flowered between them. After a while she asked Lucy the reason for her visit, and Lucy said, 'Well, you see...' and hesitated and took off her gloves.

She held her hands in the puddle of light, watching the Wise Woman's eyes to see if they would flinch or betray disgust. But the Wise Woman turned the left hand over to see the warts on the palm, and when she said nothing, just nodding as though she'd seen as many before, Lucy said: 'I've counted a hundred and nine on this hand, and eighty three on the other.'

The Wise Woman nodded and waited for Lucy to tell more; and Lucy found that the more she told, the more there was for the telling. She told how it began, over a year ago, she couldn't remember the day, it hadn't seemed important, just one small wart, and there was nothing unusual in that, was there? Then every day when she woke up, there were more, like a nightmare; she would have become a parlourmaid at Michaelmas if there hadn't been so many.

She'd tried recommended cures. Cook swore by caustic soda, and the under-gardener had said try the white fur of a broad bean pod; but none of it had helped. She'd tried the doctor, too. Then somebody had told her about the Wise Woman who could succeed where others failed. So now she was here with half-a-crown in her purse to prove she was in earnest.

The Wise Woman nodded at the mention of money. The she asked: 'You started courtin'?' And Lucy blushed and said yes, only she was so ashamed because her gloves were thin and he could feel the warts beneath.

The Wise Woman nodded again and took a tealeaf from her bottom lip. She looked at it a long time as though the tealeaf was very interesting; and what she was doing was deciding about Lucy. When she spoke, she spoke at length about how much depended on Lucy. She must do everything she was told to do at the correct times and in the correct way. Moreover she must believe, for if she did not believe there could be no help for her.

Lucy said yes, yes, she believed, and put her half-crown on the table to prove it; so the Wise Woman rose from her chair and moved heavily to a cupboard beside the fire. From there she brought out the secret which she'd inherited from her mother, who had been the finest 'White Witch' of the southern moor.

It was a silk bag containing nine leaves of heart fever grass and nine scarlet pimpernel flowers. She told Lucy to spread her hands on the table, palms downwards. Then she held the bag over them and this is what she said:

> Herb pimpernel I have thee found
> Growing on Christ Jesus' ground.
> The same gift Lord Jesu gave free
> When his blood he shed to spare thee.
> Herb grass this evil pass,
> And God bless all who wear thee.

'Amen,' said the Wise Woman.

'Amen,' said Lucy, several seconds late. Then she turned her hands palms upwards, and the Wise Woman repeated the prayer, with Lucy waiting to share the 'Amen.'

The Wise Woman gave her the bag, which Lucy must wear around her neck. Day and night, never taking it off. That was most important, but not all. Twice a day, at six in the morning and nine at night, she must hold the bag over the warts and repeat the prayer; slowly and quietly and with conviction, the way prayers were meant to be said. Would she do that?

Yes, yes, Lucy said, and had only one question. How long would it be before... before she could walk hand-in-hand, the way sweethearts do?

But the Wise Woman wouldn't say. Perhaps a week, if Lucy believed enough. Lucy nodded, for she believed with all her youth, with all her desire to be admired. And because she had nothing else to believe in, she went on believing when the warts were there after a week, a fortnight, a month. Then, on the first morning of the fifth week, they were gone, suddenly as though her hands were wiped clean. And that evening Lucy took off her glove so that she could walk hand-in-hand the way sweethearts do.

But Lucy never told anyone about the silk bag and the magic prayer; for to confess the cure would have been to confess the blemish, and that was something she wished to forget. Soon she was sure that she had never had warts at all; that the half-frightened visit to the Wise Woman had never happened.

She never went back to the lost cottage, and because of this the Wise Woman knew that the cure had been successful; for the Wise Women of seventy years ago were outside village society, mildly suspect because they had unusual powers. Only when other cures failed did men and women pocket their prejudice and fears and come to the silent door, pledging belief with half-a-crown.

*SDJ*

# Purple Harvest

Lights move in the bedroom windows. Families are dressing, shivering in the early morning and fumbling for buttons.

The lights disappear, then come back in the kitchen windows. Now the day is fully awake. A harvest day has begun.

Mrs Coombe, big and red with feet that are swollen so that her boots are ugly, calls her children and down they come; her three daughters and two sons. No school for them today. Us be gwain pickin.' And to pick on Dartmoor is to gather whortleberries by the quart.

When daylight is opening in the sky, rolling back the tent of night and taking the stars with it, they leave their cottage; Mrs Coombe big-aproned, the girls pinnafored, the boys looking for trouble if they dawn watch out.

They turn out of the village towards the green lowlands, and on the way they are joined by others. Whole families going to pick the whortleberries that make a purple harvest on the slopes.

No junketing journey this. The whortleberry harvest is serious; earning money that will take the shiver out of winter. And those which you cannot sell have their uses. Wine and tarts and jam. Good, healthy food for growing families, and children who get fed up with it can go without. You'm never finicky if you'm hungered enough, and them what idn hungered enough'll get round to it dreckly.

Mrs Coombe is one of the fastest pickers in the village, and that's no small achievement; for picking whortleberries is an art. Her short fingers, rough and red like a cat's tongue, pick more in an hour than some manage in a day.

Of this accomplishment she says: 'Shaws what you kin do when you've got to,' but truly there's more to it than that. It's a knack, learned imperceptibly from her mother. Her children have it, too. Of course the girls are the best, the quickest, the less likely to eat too many; for girls seem always to be more deft and obedient and worth their salt.

They pick without speaking or thinking. Speed is important lest the weather breaks and tomorrow be so barbed with rain that you flinch to face it. They stop for a dinner of home-baked bread and fat bacon; and go on picking until dusk.

Then, blue-splashed and tired, the tips of their fingers sore, they turn for home; moving slowly across the heedless more, their baskets heavier at every step. They do not talk. They do not sing as Italian peasants might sing. Their eyes are down in plodding. And from the children there are no protests.

They have been brought up in the knowledge that this work is necessary. That without it there will be a wolf at the door instead of winter. And experience has taught them that during these summer weeks when the berries are ripe, their mother will be short of temper; with a backhander that tolerates no argument.

So Mrs Coombe, her apron splashed as though from slaughter, comes in from the moor; her shoulders bowed and her feet sobbing. Her head feels heavy, heavy enough for sleep, but she knows that she cannot sleep, and her thoughts go round and round like horses at the fair telling her that her worries aren't over. Having picked the harvest, she must get a fair price for it. Not less than twopence a quart. More perhaps. There'll have to be more if…

She's too tired for talk now. But were she not so tired, she would say she's glad the day is over. Not only because of the work and the long journey home. But because she's in from the moor.

Tidn a woman's place. Tis a man's. And it dawn like women there. You can veel it all around.

That was the whortleberry harvest within living memory, and of course the berries still grow. But the method of harvesting has changed. Pickers come from towns on a sort of glorified day out.

Fancy prices are paid, too. More than four shillings a quart. And when prices are so high, there's none to spare for kitchen needs. But when the 'foreigners' came, the village people withdrew, suspicious and resentful. And children are seldom kept from school to work the sun down now.

*SDJ*

# Totnes and the Lower Dart

# From **PARADE OF HORSES**

## The Circus

*Totnesians trying to visualise the scene of this will have to imagine the area along Coronation Road between the borough park and the supermarket, and take away everything they can see.*

It's a patch of waste land where the irises grow. It's all that remains of the acre where the circus used to be.

Ours was a small market town, so it did not qualify for a big circus. It made do with those which toured the green country in days when the radio was wireless and films were silent and cars were as few as birds in winter. May to September was the tenting season. The circus came for two days and four performances. You could get in for sixpence, for half price if you were young enough. You could also get in for nothing, which is what I had to do.

I remember the last to come. It came from a town twelve miles away and no one believed the advance publicity, which promised a stupendous attraction. Its wagons were drawn by brown and white skewbalds and black and white piebalds with smaller ponies hitched to the back of each wagon, their feet pattering to keep up like children beside their fathers. The smallest was no more than nine hands high, instantly recognisable as the 'Joey;' the clown's pony which would butt the ringmaster and steal his hat and represent mischief to a young audience.

The wagons were driven by the father and his two sons. Mother and daughters sat beside them; dark haired and brown, not

95

recognisable as the girls who would become tight-rope walkers and acrobats and bare-back riders. We walked beside the wagons to the patch of waste land, half afraid of the circus family because they were foreign and had foreign skills, yet fascinated by what they represented. They represented something denied to us by school walls and empty pockets and parental authority. They represented freedom, by which we meant new places and staying up late and getting away from the neighbours.

They seemed not to notice us or care about our fascination. They drove the wagons to a corner of the waste land and got down swiftly. No orders were given by the father or needed by his sons and daughters. They knew what to do while the mother remained in the wagon, fat and busy and sometimes singing. It was a strange song. It seemed to come out of the long ago, when nomad families first took their performing animals across Europe.

The sons released the horses from the shafts and tethered them on long ropes for grazing. This evening piebalds and skewbalds would become 'rosin-backs,' the name of the stuff which trickriders use to give their feet a firmer grip. But the ponies were not tethered. They wandered with lengths of rope dangling from their necks. When one stepped on a rope it was momentarily checked and this frequent interruption reminded it that it was only on parole. The Joey had no rope. He grazed alone, his ears flattening if you came near. You could see that the impudent comedian which audiences were meant to love was in private petulant and moody.

Two terriers lay in the shade of a wagon. This evening they would play a kind of tennis, bouncing a ball across a low net and barking in excitement as they reached for the high ones. Until then they would remain tethered as sheepdogs are confined to ensure their keenness when they are released. I felt sorry for the dogs and remembered what my mother had said about circus animals living 'unnatural lives,' compelled to do 'unnatural tricks' and governed by fear. Yet when I ventured close enough to see their faces, the terriers did not seem cowed or afraid. They were watching the daughter who had trained them, their eyes bright and ears awake, like collies which wait for the whistle.

The tent breathed up and the sons hammered stakes while the daughters fixed wooden tiers around the ring in readiness for a full house. I wanted to warn them. The day was Friday, pay-day for the workers of saw mill and corn mill, and therefore a good day, but the town wasn't impressed by what the circus family had to offer. They were out of date. I'd heard my parents say so. Our town had a picture-house now and some families had the wireless. We no longer needed the old tricks and familiar clowning which were all a small circus could offer.

At midday the circus family gathered on the steps of a wagon and ate and drank, talking seldom, smelling of sunshine and dust and tiredness. The father sat on the top step, his hair grey and his face deeply lined; seeming no different from the tired men of our town yet made different by his skills, by his freedom from rates and neighbours and bosses, by the rootlessness which meant that although he knew everywhere, he belonged nowhere, always on the outside of the small towns. Once he might have been a juggler and acrobat, apparently fearless on the trapeze. In his middle years he might have been a clown. Now he had passed those accomplishments on to his sons and was the boss, which meant he was also ringmaster and horsemaster, farrier and veterinary surgeon. His veterinary treatment needed to be quick if the circus was to be kept moving.

When a horse had a poisoned foot, he covered bread with boiling water and placed the steaming pulp in a sack, drawing it over the hoof and tying it around the leg. If the injury was a bruised tendon he led the horse to a stream and stood beside it in the shallows, stroking its long sad face as the cold fanned around the leg and reduced the swelling. Every day brought its crisis and every day he had to find an answer without spending money. Today it was a wagon wheel and he had to be a wheelwright.

The sons helped him repair it while the mother and daughters scrubbed clothes and hung them on lines between wagons. They seemed remarkably disciplined and humble, much more versatile than those of the town who condemned them vagrants and illiterates. I inched closer, making it plain that I didn't want only to get in for nothing.

They let me help with the horses. The sunshine which warmed the girls' laundry and blessed the hayfields was savage to the horses. They aimed their tails and shook their manes, but the black flies of

97

summer do not only harass. They bite and raise great lumps, clustering in the corners of a horse's eyes and drinking the tears. Horseflies, as brown as shreds of old leaf, pierce the skin and suck blood. They are disgusting things and it's a merciful hand which swipes them.

I stood near the oldest rosinback, swatting and counting and making great gestures in the air. He knew what I was doing and leaned closer, rubbing his tears against my shoulder when I had to wait a minute because my arm was dropping off. Halfway through the afternoon two others came near enough to benefit from the service, but the Joey wanted help from none. He crept to the side of a wagon and kept his tail sniping. Meanwhile other ponies formed their own community, standing nose-to-tail so that the tail of one cleaned the face of another.

You knew it was nearly time when the ponies came towards the wagons, as punctual for the first performance as cows for milking. They had decorations on their surcingles and bridles, but sunlight exposed the shoddiness and took all pretence of splendour out of the plumes which the rosinbacks wore to make them seem taller. I began to wonder how long the family could continue. They must have known the days of the small circus were almost over, yet there was no surrender in their talk. The younger daughter was asking when she could attempt in public the back-somersault which she had achieved in private. Her father said not yet, as though there was plenty of time.

He put on the hat which was the symbol of authority and which a clown would knock off for the Joey to steal. The Joey came fussily towards the tent, shaking his bells to claim attention. The mother dressed the dogs. They wore green skirts and the dog which always won leered at the girl who had trained them, eager for the game to begin. Sons came from the caravan, transformed by grotesque paint and ginger wigs, by clown clothes which had water-jets in the lapels and trick flowers in the pockets. The daughters wore tinselled skirts and had paper flowers in their hair. One of them took the dogs; the other rubbed her satin shoes in rosin like a boxer before the first round. Their mother came to her place at the flap. They waited for the customers.

I wanted to explain but they didn't look at me. They looked up the hill and waited twenty minutes. Their faces showed neither surprise nor humiliation, but I felt their contempt of those who supposed that shadows on a screen and voices in a box could be a substitute for living skills. The sons and daughters watched their father, waiting for him to decide. He waited five more minutes, then beckoned the mother to raise the flap, the younger daughter to bring the rosinbacks. He passed into the tent and cracked his whip and the rosinbacks began to go round and round, their strides matched, as monotonous as jaws chewing gum.

The sons came to the centre of the ring, calling encouragement to their sister as she ran beside the leading horse and sprang and sat and stood and raised a leg, performing elementary tricks in preparation, her face pale, a corner of her mouth creased in a tremor, her brothers crying wordless sounds like warriors as she slid from the broad back and retreated until she was standing beside her father in the centre of the ring. She needed a roll of drums to celebrate the tightening of her courage. I was near enough to see the sweat on her top lip.

Her father cracked the whip and the rosinbacks went round twice while she leaned and waited, waited too long, running forward and faltering and coming back to her father who was ready to call it off if she wasn't sure. She shook her head and leaned again, beginning to run while the leading rosinback was several strides away. She reached it and swung and rose and straightened, fiddling her feet backward until she was standing between loins and hip, her arms out on either side, her body breathing with the rhythm.

Her mother made the sign of the cross as she watched from the flap. Her brothers looked up, their anxieties showing through the grinning paint. Her father watched the horses. They all trusted the horses. If one of them faltered or changed its stride, she would fall and break her back.

The horses were concentrating, their heads drawn in by short side reins, their eyes down, only their ears moving to show they were waiting for the instant of decision. The girl decided. Her body rose and began to turn. The arc seemed not to be high enough or brave enough. The soft young body seemed doomed and for a moment quicker than a blink, I imagined her sprawling, as broken as a bird. But she made it, somehow she made it. Her feet found the back of the second horse, her body wobbled, her arms went out; the fright in her face showed how close she was to falling. She swayed and stayed there while her brothers cheered and her mother clapped and the rosinbacks pounded a rhythm which seemed to quicken in relief.

It wasn't a new trick. It had been performed by Cossacks and Hungarians, perhaps by the Persians eight thousand years ago; but her panting made it seem new, a wonderful achievement. She circled the ring twice, holding out her arms to the empty benches, then sliding down and running to her father.

She was his favourite. I sensed that in the subtle something which passed between them; a matching of smiles as though triumph had been created out of the nothing which the town had given. The rosinbacks slowed and stopped and nodded their plumes. She palmed each a cube of sugar. She was still patting them when the dressed-up dogs came dancing in with jubilation.

It was the only performance which this family gave in our town. In the morning they hitched the horses which had been rosinbacks and the town watched them go with relief, because even those with wirelesses felt guilty about the empty tent. Few remember them now, but when I come to the place where the irises grow like flowers on a grave, I wonder what happened to the father who had to be veterinary surgeon and farrier and wheelwright; to the sons who had inherited a dying tradition; to the mother who had clapped. I wonder most about the daughter, if she ever repeated that trick to the applause of a hot and crowded tent. You fall in love easily when you are ten and I think I must have fallen in love with her when I realised her fright and how close she was to falling.

Perhaps that's why I remember the horses which saved her; remember them so clearly that for me the king of circus horses is not the high school specialist or the Arab stallion or the Joey pony running off with someone's hat and everyone's laughter. It is the trustworthy rosinback, pounding round and round with head drawn in and eyes serious, waiting for the moment of decision.

# Working in Pairs

They had difficulty getting it down the stairs. It was long and heavy and the stairs bent sharply like an arm. Those in front panted orders to those behind, their voices hushed because this was the coffin and the mourners were listening and the hearse was at the door.

The man who was suddenly a coffin had been a horseman. Framed photographs of horses were on the walls of his kitchen and the foot of a favourite horse was his favourite ornament. His last request had been for an old-fashioned funeral. No motor hearse with cars following; but black horses with black plumes and the coachman wearing black gloves.

They gave him what he wanted. It was the last horse-drawn funeral to be seen in our town and what I remember is the slowness of the horses, their natural gaiety subdued, their eyes down in what seemed to be deference. They'd known what would be required of them as soon as they'd seen the black plumes, the black crepe on the bridles. You couldn't recognise them as the pair which also drew the fire engine.

The fire engine was owned by the town and staffed by volunteers who wore helmets which shone like the brass instruments in the town band. It was kept in a shed near the market and the volunteers were summoned by the ringing of tenor and treble bells. Everyone recognised the peculiar ding-dong from the church tower and the wives of volunteers were supposed to sleep lightly so that they could awaken the heroes and find their uniforms, sometimes helping with the buttons or finding the hatchet. Our brigade was proud of its speed of turn-out.

Seven volunteers ran to the shed which was called the fire station, while the eighth ran to the mews where the horses were stabled. The undertaker lived above the stables. The volunteer found him fumbling his braces and panting questions, frightened by the bells bouncing their sounds across the roofs.

The horses came out with eyes wild and nostrils flaring, catching the sounds of running, perhaps the smell of smoke. The undertaker ran behind them to the fire station, holding the long reins and almost stepping on the traces. Half the town helped to back them and fasten them, to hold the doors wide as the undertaker became the fire engine driver and clambered to his perch. Someone clanged the bell. The horses leapt and the volunteers clung, thinking ten miles an hour fast as the vehicle swung out of the market square towards the red stain in the sky.

Sometimes the fire was a barn ten miles away, and when the engine got there the volunteers were frustrated because the hoses were not long enough or the stream deep enough. Often the horses did not come back till morning, when they ceased to be fire horses and became carriage horses, booked to meet the train from Paddington and to convey guests to the town's best hotel.

One of the pair was a former steeplechaser, which had almost run in the Grand National of 1922. He had damaged his forelegs in a preliminary race and been retired from racing, a virtual cripple until the undertaker of our town bought him cheaply and kept him trotting the roads. Men used to say, as they watched the carriage pass, that this horse might be fully restored by steady trotting, might even race again and bring honour to the town. It wasn't as implausible as it sounded, for the American-bred Rubio had won the Grand National of 1908 after breaking down more than three years before. In those years Rubio had drawn the hotel bus from the railway station at Towcester to the Prospect Arms and back again, earning his keep while trotting hardness into his legs. We schoolboys looked ahead to it happening again, but it did not. Perhaps our horse was not good enough. More probably he was too old.

Another pair of horses drew the carrier's cart which was the only link that isolated villages had with the market town. The cart was heavy and the passengers sat on either side, facing each other with baskets and hampers, perhaps with a calf half-trussed by sacking in the space between their knees. They began the journey with excited small talk, for the journey to market was a big event and there was always plenty to tell. But the talk frayed away as the horses plodded and the big wheels rumbled. Heads became heavy and drooped like flowers, jolting awake when the wagon stopped at a wayside cottage and new voices approached. Six miles an hour was considered fair. Men got out on the hills and an iron shoe braked a wheel during steep descents.

The horses had broad backs, and bells on their harness, and were known to passengers by their names. Bella and Daisy worked together for twenty years, as famous locally as a music-hall act. They served the villages which branch-line railways neglected and were still the only means of public transport when the first bus crept nervously towards the hills in the early 1920s.

Some of the best horses in the neighbourhood were bought by hauliers for the regular transport of bulk supplies to and from factories; for the hauling of trucks along railway sidings to piers where ships were loading. The best hauliers had great, dappled Percherons, originally bred by farmers in the Le Perche district of France and regarded with awe like heavyweight boxers. Women called them the 'Gentle Giants.' The man who drove and cared for them, as dedicated as a priest, loved them for their willingness, their nobility and - not least - for their clean legs.

Percherons have no long hair (or feather) around their lower legs, so the evening task of cleaning was made simpler for the Percheron man than for the Clydesdale man, who loved his Clydesdales and would admit no fault in them, yet whose working day was made longer by the need to clean the long, white hair on each leg and foot. This was no easy task in winter, when Clydesdales had been hauling through mud. There was a saying among other horsemen that you needed to be a saint to work with Clydesdales and like it.

Another haulier preferred the Suffolk Punch, bred in East Anglia since 1506 and famous for its strength in a direct pull. People came to the pavements to watch our pair of chestnut Punches working with a kind of furious majesty, their ears sharp for the voice which walked beside them when the hill was cruel. Good horsemen used their voices to encourage, then to call for more during the final yards; like the pack leader of rugby forwards when they push over for a try. Some horsemen scorned the use of whips and sometimes the use of reins. Towns were proud of those who walked yards away, calling instructions with the certainty that the horses would not miss a word.

The wise haulier, having invested in the best, supervised their feeding with fanatical care. Eighteen pounds of oats a day were not unusual, the grain slightly crushed by hand-machine to assist the process of mastication, perhaps dampened as well to make mastication easier. Some horsemen, catching the fanaticism of their employers, used eggs to dampen, robbing their own hen-houses despite the protests of their wives. Six eggs a day were not too many. Bantam eggs were considered as nutritious as hen eggs. One horseman kept hens and bantams for no other purpose. I remember his son saying that his family never had eggs for breakfast.

Hay had to be old yet sweet, without dust when you shook it. Hauliers differed most in their choice of hay, but all were agreed that meadow hay could not be hard enough. Mixtures of rye grass and red clover gave the right hard muscle shine. It was fed from the rack or chopped into chaff. It also supplied the essential roughage and, because of its importance to the teams, the hay harvest was crucial to the haulier as well as to farmers in the neighbourhood.

Oats and hay were the basic foods but some hauliers added supplementaries, including black treacle and chopped carrots and watercress and fish oils. The one I knew best was cranky about dandelions, insisting they were not only a source of iron but a delicacy which stabled horses greeted with delight.

It was true. Their nostrils trembled when you came in with the green stuff, their natural courtesy suspended as they nudged and fussed, grudging the time necessary to chop the roots and shred the leaves, to break the stems and expose the juices. I didn't know then that this haulier had borrowed his crankiness from stonecutters in the long ago who had dug dandelions from the hedgerows to supplement their bread and cheese, biting the roots as a substitute for radish and getting accustomed to the hot sting.

He also believed that everything which horses needed could be found in hedgerows if you had gypsy eyes and knew where to look. He encouraged me to gather blackberry leaves, regardless of fingers sore from prickles; nut leaves when they were young and green, before autumn began to toughen them; fat thistles with the juices dribbling. It shocked me that horses which had the best could take thistles delicately into their mouths and squeeze out the juices with delight reflected in their eyes. I'd supposed thistles to be tramp food, suitable only for donkeys.

Not all hauliers could afford the best horses; not all mills and factories would pay the fees which the best hauliers needed to charge. Minor hauliers bought cheap horses and fed them poorly, reducing costs in order to keep prices low. This was considered good business during the bleak years of the late 1920s, when the plight of overworked horses seemed less urgent than the plight of families whose fathers were unemployed. But occasionally the conscience of the town was stricken by the ugly spectacle of horses struggling, going to their knees in a kind of entreaty as their back feet slipped and the wheels slid while the driver used the whip with the cruelty of panic, appalled by what would happen if the wagon slid further or the load toppled.

The town knew it wasn't the driver's fault; that he would lose his job if he begged for smaller loads or more time or for an extra horse on the steep hills. Yet spectators focussed their anger on him because they were not sure who else to blame. Occasionally the incident was reported and the driver and haulier appeared before magistrates, some of whom were also mill owners and factory owners, vitally interested in keeping prices down. Perhaps their indignation was assumed. Perhaps it was genuine, as though to sit on a Bench is to acquire another identity. But everyone knew that the driver and haulier were not alone in guilt. Any sentence could only be a partial justice and the wisest constable of our town knew it.

He didn't bother with notebook and pencil. He unhooked the wooden block from the back of the wagon and wedged it beneath a wheel; holding the weight for a time, giving the horses partial respite in the hope that, with all the men coming from the pavements to lend their strengths and himself taking the lead horse from the frightened driver, he could get the wagon climbing and the life of the town moving. This constable was never promoted, perhaps because he did not keep his notebook full; but he was respected in our town, not least by those who liked horses.

There was another pair which appeared occasionally, drawing a long, low vehicle like a bathchair and driven by a lady whose legs were always wrapped in rugs. But we didn't take this pair seriously, for they were donkeys, at the bottom of the class in schoolboy language, their ears flapping like a jester's cap, their eyes slanted and inscrutable. We believed donkeys to be peasant animals and couldn't understand why a lady preferred them to horses. Our parents couldn't understand it either. They implied that such perversity was permissible only because the lady was rich, so we had to mind our manners and keep straight faces when the penny-sized hooves trotted by.

I wish now that I'd taken those donkeys seriously and had scraped acquaintance with the lady whose legs were always hidden. She might have had much to tell me about their intelligence, their capacity for affection which can be as loyal as a dog's. In another way donkeys are like cats, inclined to consider what you want, then to decide if it is worth doing. If it isn't, their obstinacy can be humiliating; which is why experienced horsemen used to say that if you can drive a donkey, you can drive anything. Presumably the lady in the grey hat could have driven anything, for she handled her donkeys with ease.

They were a jack and Jenny. The Jack was darker and slightly taller but the Jenny was boss, which seemed right to women watching from the pavement. The pair made three stops in our long High Street: at the pastry cook's, where the proprietor came out with a cardboard box which set young imaginations wondering; at the book shop, where the pages of *The Strand* magazine smelled as new as varnish; and at the bank on the corner, which had pillars like a temple and a kind of hush. At no time did the driver get out. She was met by senior assistants whose deference made it plain that she was rich enough to be important. I think they were embarrassed by the donkeys.

But an old man of the town was wiser. He called them the 'Jesus pair' and at once I saw Jerusalem and the cheering faces of Palm Sunday, when Christ rode the humblest of animals towards the shadow of the Cross. I think the old lady knew what the old man called them, for occasionally their glances met in a smile of understanding.

# The Races

*Vian has renamed and rearranged some of the Totnes hostelries here; earlier in the book the London Inn, with its old coaching associations, sounds like the Royal Seven Stars, but here it is at the top of the 'long, steep street,' so perhaps Loppy stayed at the Bay Horse or Bull. There was never a London Inn or Saracen's Head in Totnes, but the Waterman's Arms and Lord Nelson are with us still. The racecourse lies beneath the industrial estate.*

My first racehorse was a small bay with big knees and sad eyes, and what I remember best are his ears. They were long and limp and because they drooped when he was pensive, race day crowds thought he was stupid. I wish he could have confounded derision by winning in a canter, telling the mockers to take it out of that; but in the years of our acquaintance he never won anything and seemed not to think he could.

He was mine for three days a year when he came to our town for the September meeting and was stabled at the London Inn, where stage-coaches had pulled in a hundred years before. There were stables on the race course but not enough to accommodate all the horses which would run in twelve races. Those which could not be accommodated there were sent to stables in the town; some of which were supposed to be dark slums. But the London Inn was proud of its stables and of the coaching history which they represented. A week before the meeting, when the landlord knew how many horses were coming, the litter which had accumulated during the year was broomed out and walls were whitewashed, troughs scrubbed, doors made new with creosote.

Provision of straw for bedding was the landlord's responsibility and he made that responsibility a pride. It was always wheat straw, less edible and more absorbent than that of oat or barley. One of the old men who lived in a corner of the bar, never seeming to eat as though he needed only pipe and pint, was employed by the landlord to prepare each bed with out-dated skill.

He placed the straw in a criss-cross pattern that urine would leak through and leave the top straw clean. In those days, when corn was harvested by reaper and handled with respect, wheat straw was never less than nine inches long and one of the incidental skills of the stableman was this criss-cross pattern done with such swift economy that it seemed easy. The straw was thickest around the walls, forming high cushions to protect legs and back when the horse lay down or to prevent him becoming cast if he rolled.

A horse can rise only by straightening his forelegs. If he rolls so near a wall that his forelegs cannot straighten, he is a semi-prisoner and will struggle, wrenching muscles and inflicting internal injuries which might be difficult to treat or even to diagnose. A horse is most likely to become *cast* when he is in a strange stable, and might struggle for hours before the top door opens and somebody looks in. By then he is exhausted and unable to race for days.

My favourite old man, whose pipe trembled between his gums, told me this in a mumble as he billowed the straw. He liked to talk as he worked, and it was through him that I heard about the old days, when horses walked from meeting to meeting, ignoring the railways as dangerous and expensive. Steady exercise was good for their feet and legs, healthier or at any rate cheaper than confinement in a truck. They walked from twenty to thirty miles a day, sometimes grazing at nights near the road while their lads improvised beds out of coats and slept like cowboys, each with a saddle for his pillow.

I wondered what had happened when it rained, but you weren't supposed to ask questions. You were supposed to believe that such Spartan travel had kept horses tough. Their legs slicked by dew, their feet kept hard by walking; making them less prone to injuries than the pampered thoroughbreds of modern times and much less afflicted by boredom.

The old man believed boredom to be as harmful to the horse as it is to people; that it encourages mischief of the mind, expressed by horses in crib-biting and wind-sucking, by tail-rubbing and a restless weaving. He thought horses should come hungry to their trough and tired to their bed.

His prejudice over-simplified the problems of keeping horses fit, but there was good sense behind it. Walking never hurt a horse while short periods of grazing stimulate its appetite for dry artificial foods. Boredom is a burden to an animal confined for about twenty-two hours a day and as many injuries are inflicted during these periods of boredom as during the hours of work. He was right to insist that the racehorse of the nineteenth century was tougher than its modern counterpart, capable of running twice in an afternoon and winning twice; but what he omitted to stress was the change in standards. Small races of the nineteenth century were slow, capable of being won by part-breds and by hunters which would be considered out-classed a hundred years later.

Two hours before the horses arrived the stables were new and exciting; the walls as white as surplices, emphasising the yellowness of straw and darkness of creosote. The creosote was not only a gesture towards proper maintenance. It gave the wood a bitter taste, sufficient to discourage all save the most perverse from random gnawing.

If you kept quiet and believed everything the old man said, you were allowed to broom the yard, where coaches had stood while ostlers had changed teams. Windows of the inn still looked down like theatre boxes to a stage and faces were still at the lattice, speculating about what horses would come and if they would win, arguing about the great year when horses from the London Inn had won eight races in two days, showering riches on the customers, none of whom dared admit he'd backed something else.

The horses came by train. Boys of the town were at the station to watch it steam in and shrug off the boxes. A shunting engine, nicknamed Puffing Billy, shunted the boxes to a siding where hatch doors opened and the lads appeared.

They were always lads in stable jargon, although some were grey and wizened. Others were semi-gypsies, wild of hair and dark of tan; what my mother called 'race day roughs' who slept beside their horses either in drunken stupor or because their employers, called their masters by racing authorities, refused to pay two shillings a night for a bed. Some were Irish. Some were orphanage lads, compelled at fourteen to find a substitute for home in licensed stables, where discipline was cruder than in the Services but made tolerable by the prospect of sudden reward. The lad who 'did' a good horse could expect gifts from a grateful owner. If he was denied a good horse and had to make do with screws and nags and scrubbers, there was always the hope of picking up 'whispers' like a radio sensitive to unseen voices. If the 'whispers' were right, he could turn shillings into pounds; making more in ten minutes than a skilled craftsman earned in a month. This seemed madness to my mother and to those craftsmen who backed losers.

Elder lads, those with grey hair and an ingrained contempt of the young, were as elegant as the grooms of private stables; their boots and leggings polished to a brown shine, their shirt sleeves rolled meticulously to their elbows. They were expert in the rolling of sleeves; for some reason despising sleeves cut short, using their tight and tidy rolling to reproach young lads who were sloppy and without pride.

Two horses for the Lord Nelson Inn were unloaded. We watched the lads pass out sacks of oats and trusses of hay, the hamper which contained paddock sheets and night-rugs and brushes. A railway uniform, helping in the hope of picking up a 'whisper,' which would prove more valuable than a formal tip, transferred the miscellany to the cart of the town porter; stacking it in a corner to ensure sufficient space for the sacks and hampers which would be taken to other inns.

There were stories of the town porter confusing the consignments, delivering hay at the London which should have gone to the Waterman's, thereby provoking jealous fighting among the lads and prejudicing the outcome of races. I began to understand that it was not enough to have hay. It had to be the type to which the horse had become accustomed. A sudden change could worry a potential winner. One trainer, making water as important as hay, insisted that his horses were accompanied by churns, filled at their home pump. A horse drinks about eight gallons a day, so each of his horses needed two twelve gallon churns to cover the period of a meeting. Three or four horses could mean as many as eight churns, which made railway uniforms groan and the town porter mutinous.

The town porter wore a peaked cap and smelled of snuff. His horse was a grey which had turned white in old age. It moved away as the racehorses appeared, like the humble moving from royalty. Boys of the town habitually derided its dipped back and tragic bones, but on the eve of a race meeting, when its poverty was emphasised by the shine of thoroughbreds, the joke became sour. We felt sorry for it as it plodded towards the town, distributing better food than ever it had tasted.

Some horses wore leather pads to protect their knees. Others had rubber pads between their ears, protecting sensitive polls from random blows when trucks were being shunted. Railway staffs were supposed to take special care of horses during transit, but we'd seen what happened to calves in hessian and chicks in boxes, to homing pigeons in hampers. We though trainers were right to take elaborate precautions.

The horses came down the ramps with more curiosity than apprehension. Some were hurdlers, with small heads and sharp ears. A few were steeplechasers, their withers high and their legs long, their travelling bandages hiding the scars of firing. Experienced lads handled them casually, always on a long leading rein. You could tell the inexperienced by his need to grasp the rein by the head-collar.

Sometimes professionals needed help. A lad with three horses could not lead them simultaneously. He needed help from town boys, giving them the honour of leading the probable winner of the second race on Wednesday or the veteran which had fallen in the Grand National of 1931 and would run in the three-mile steeplechase on Thursday. He walked in front, looking back to the volunteers, shouting to the 'townie' who was leading on the off side and with his left hand, rebuking him because it confused the horse which was accustomed to being led on the near side and by the right hand. Sometimes he called back questions, asking which way to the Waterman's. There were few cars or motor vans in the early 1930s and they immediately conceded right of way. The greatest hazard was the blue bus which once an hour came to the square. It was the only vehicle which felt important enough to challenge the ancient right of horses.

I waited for those destined for the London Inn. Three came out with heads high and feet lilting, their bandaged tails extended in what seemed to be banners of pride. The fourth to appear was small and dull and perpetually preoccupied, sliding down the ramp and waiting for something to happen like a browned-off soldier who has travelled too often. This was mine. I approached him with what amounted to a handshake, making it a kind of reunion which at least one of us appreciated. Railway uniforms called him Old Loppy because of his ears and it is by this name that I remember him; although racecards pretended he was Prince Something, a remote descendant of The Tetrarch and St Simon, with others in his pedigree which were to racing what the Cecils were to the House of Lords.

A junior lad, with black hair and gypsy eyes and Killarney in his voice, took the first horse. The senior lad, who wore a yellow waistcoat and brown breeches, with a tweed cap to deny his baldness, followed with two others. I was in the middle with the dunce. We proceeded in triumph from the railway to the town, bringing people from shops and kitchens, men from ladders as they asked the names of the horses and if their time had come for winning.

There was a strong belief among workmen that while racing was 'The Sport of Kings,' it was also corrupt. Minor hurdle races and steeplechases were believed to be so 'fixed' that almost every horse achieved victory during the season; by which amiable arrangement small trainers were able to stay in business while the owner of a mediocre horse could make a profit by backing it only when success was guaranteed.

This arrangement could never have been as amiable as the credulous supposed, but belief that it existed invested accident or error with sinister undertones. If the favourite fell at the last fence, it was not an accident and the jockey was only feigning injury. It was part of a deliberate plot to allow the 20-1 outsider to win. Or if a horse ran out at a fence or swerved through a wing or passed the wrong side of a marking flag or was brought down by other fallers; if it refused at the open ditch or was pulled up without obvious signs of injury, clever faces in the crowd immediately smelled corruption and for weeks afterwards men in overalls described how it had been done and why, mourning less the corruption than the secrecy which had excluded them.

But on the day before a meeting there was no suspicion; only a rising excitement, sharpened by the prospect of sheaves of fivers which would prove that racing was honest after all. There were even those who asked about Loppy. Would he win tomorrow> If the question was aimed at me, my response was always a smiling silence; implying a trickery too deep to be casually revealed. What wounded me most was for Loppy to be ignored. On these occasions I whispered to him to do something, somehow to prove himself; imagining the consternation if he won by twenty lengths from the astonished favourite. Every year the dream seemed plausible during the long walk to the London Inn.

Loppy had the box in a corner, where the sun never reached. He walked in without surprise or protest, lowering his head to breathe questions over the straw, then looking around for hay and water. When he was sure about them he chose his place and stared at me in concentration, his body stiffening as he widened his hind legs and passed urine. By this act he put his smell into the box and made it his. He always did it within minutes, but the senior lad told me of horses which fretted for hours, unable to pass their mark. There were even those which could never do it in a strange box. Their racing had to be restricted to meetings which they could reach within hours.

Old Loppy always stood and dreamed while I brushed him, awakening only when the brush passed between his front legs which was his ticklish place. He seemed to be remarkably sensible, but the conduct of others persuaded me that this was not how a fit racehorse should behave. The horse next door was writhing and snapping, earning the reproaches and simultaneously the respect of the Irish lad. It began to lurch its back legs, kicking the partition in thuds which rose and kept rising until they were higher than my head. This was supposed to be the exuberance of a potential winner, but I cringed and thanked heaven for Loppy.

Faces came from the windows to inspect. It was important that horses stabled at the London Inn should win more races than those stabled at the Lord Nelson and Waterman's Arms and Saracen's Head. Prestige as well as silver was at stake. The faces asked questions but the lads confided little; only that the horses had been 'brought up from grass' in the middle of July and were in their sixth week of work. I gathered they were not yet fully fit and had come to our meeting only to get 'wound up' for more valuable races in the autumn. But the faces didn't believe it. They remembered last year when horses recently 'brought up' had won four races in two days.

The lads worked quickly, with their coats off and sleeves rolled; hissing between their teeth, fretting their brushes against curry combs and tapping white dust from the crevices. They were always hurrying. Their footsteps gabbled as they brought buckets and hay, tipped corn into troughs for the largest meal of the day. By six o'clock top doors were closed and bolted, ostentatiously padlocked by the senior lad who retained the keys. Loppy was given the broken lock, which would open if you tapped it.

The lads departed to wash at the pump and to change their shirts, emerging spick-and-span in the bar where the landlord had drinks drawn in readiness. I was free to wander the yard, guarding Loppy from the crime which I'd read about. Nat Gould was the racing novelist of those days. He wrote about doping and crime rings, and my evening was given to frightening myself with imaginary perils. Usually I had to be sent home by the landlord.

It was a long night, spent waiting for dawn and the excuse to be up and running to the yard where Loppy's top door was the last to open. He came to the half door and blew his nostrils and waited politely, betraying no jealousy when two of the other horses were saddled and ridden to the field called Sanctuary. They were cantered briefly in what the senior lad called a 'pipe-opener.' When they came back, they were accompanied by a dapper little man who wore his soft hat at a perky angle. He was the trainer. I gathered he had arrived the previous evening and had booked at the town's largest hotel. He watched the horses being watered for the last time and given a light breakfast of bruised oats. They would not drink or eat again until their races were over.

The windows of the inn watched the trainer closely, trying to read his manner, to guess if he was pleased. At eleven o'clock the owners appeared with their wives and daughters. There were small conferences in corners of the yard and the windows strained to hear. But Loppy's owner never came. The horse was made conspicuous by neglect, like the hospital patient who receives no visitors.

The windows deduced what they could from the arrival of the farrier; one of the four blacksmiths who shod the town's vanners and carriers. He removed iron shoes and substituted steel plates: each weighing five ounces, twice as heavy as aluminium yet much lighter than iron. The horses knew what the plating signalled. They sidled and kicked, stinging the farrier's face with their tails. It was the landlord's task to keep strangers from the yard, to pretend not to know which were being plated. They never plated Loppy. He ran all his races with iron shoes, worn as thin as sixpences.

Twelve o'clock on race day was a special time. You could feel the hurry as building workers took off overalls, as women hurried from shops and girls from factories and clerks from offices. Some shops were preparing to close, making an afternoon of sport more important than the possibility of selling shoes or kettles, but those owned by Methodists and Congregationalists and Wesleyans and Plymouth Brethren never did, because racing was gambling and gambling was a sin. Moreover, hundreds were coming from the rural district and each was a potential customer. The Plymouth Brother who was also the barber was always busy on race days, for rural workers would not go to the races until their hair was cut and smelling of brilliantine.

My father hurried with a long stride. If he backed winners this afternoon, he would attend again tomorrow. Otherwise the first half-day of the meeting was his only holiday of the year apart from Bank Holidays. He was a prudent man and hated racing because he hated losing; but he also loved it because he loved winning and the excitement in his face when he won four and ninepence made it plain to me that this was special money, subtly different from four and nine earned by his tools. He was a carpenter and a good one. He wanted me to be the same and wouldn't listen when I wanted to be a jockey.

I wanted this most on race days. The rest of the year I was prepared to settle for groom or coachman or van driver. I didn't much care as long as it guaranteed work with horses, but my father kept sawing and planning, refusing to listen to anything except a trade. If he knew about Loppy and my part in race days, he gave no sign.

My part became public an hour before the race, when I was given the greatest honour of my year. The senior lad brushed Loppy and blanketed him and painted his feet with oil. He clipped a leading tape to the off side bit-ring, passed it through the near side and gave it to me, making Loppy mine for perhaps fifteen minutes. We passed solemnly down the street towards the racecourse, me talking to him without saying a word, Loppy answering with his ears; a communion of silence which sometimes brought our heads together like the back row of the cinema on Saturday nights.

He showed no fear of traffic, retiring politely to the gutter as the blue bus approached. Even the funfair, which occupied the acre where the small circus had been, did not interest him. He passed it without a glance, seeming to be preoccupied by something very deep. Through the trees I could see the bobbing caps which said that a race was being run. There were red and white flags, white rails, birch fences as neatly trimmed as suburban hedges; but Loppy had seen too many racecourses. He went towards racing like an absent-minded professor towards a classroom.

We followed other horses to the gate. You needed no official pass in those days; no passport photograph or signature or proof of identity. To be leading a horse was enough. Gates opened all the way to the paddock and this was my reward; for I could not have bought a place among the bowler hats and tweeds and shooting-sticks.

The junior lad took over, flashing complaint because I was late. I watched the trainer sponge Loppy's eyes and nostrils; place number cloth and weight cloth; tighten the girths of the lightweight saddle and pass a surcingle over it. The jockey was an Irish boy, a novice soon to become famous. When he needed to lose weight, he slept in a manure heap, using its heat to sweat off pounds as more sophisticated professionals used the Turkish bath. Presumably one of the purposes which Loppy served was giving experience to promising apprentices.

Five minutes before the advertised time of the race he was walking around the ring, still solemn and preoccupied, content to be last of eight even during the preliminaries.

The racecourse was a former wilderness near the river. It was shaped like an O which has been sat on and the stretch near the river seemed far away and empty, occupied only by ambulance uniforms and by families who picnicked between races, the mothers knitting while their children ran imitation races. Bookmakers were near the stand and crowds approached them with hands lifted, like sinners at a revivalist meeting pleading for salvation. I watched them exchange silver for tickets and place the tickets carefully in their pockets and caps. Their hurry was nervous. They'd been warned about pickpockets and bag-snatchers. They'd read about razor gangs. Their faces seemed different from those in a street; for faces in a street have many thoughts while these had only one.

The stand which seemed so august was only a series of wooden tiers, its roof supported by wooden pillars which obscured your view. I envied the bowler hats their places of privilege and found another near the rail, leaning to see the horses come to the track. They seemed many, for eight was a large field. Loppy was fourth as they walked by, chewing his bit and looking down like one who has lost something but cannot remember where. When they turned at the end of the parade, he did not throw up his head or plunge or pretend enthusiasm. His response was mechanical. He cantered past with his ears flopping and I called to him without speaking, begging him to show them.

It was a race of two miles and eight hurdles. The hurdles were three feet six inches high, made of gorse on wooden frames which leaned; ready to be knocked down by fore legs or dragged down by hind legs. The jockeys' colours made a ragged line and waited for the starters' flag. The sound from the stand, a wordless mumble like the grumble of the sea, told you that the flag had fallen, that the colours were advancing although you couldn't see or hear. Seconds passed before you heard the drumming and the breathing, the clatter of hooves on wood as they jumped the first. They came into view on your right and suddenly you didn't want to see. Loppy had ceased to be a ten-year-old gelding with big knees. He'd become a red cap and the red cap was in the middle of the tumult. I imagine him bumped by horses on either side, struck into by horses behind. For the first time I realised how he hated it.

They turned towards the river and took their sounds with them, compelling you to wait and wonder, to suffer in your imagination and at the same time to hope, because it might be different today. It never was. Once Loppy fell in the silence near the river, reappearing without his jockey and looking for the paddock as though for a welcome. Usually he found gaps in the hurdles and survived, returning only thirty seconds late to an ironic cheer. The jockey slid down with a growl of disgust and dragged off the saddle, abandoning him to the junior lad who smeared his sweat with warm water, half doing it because there was another horse in the next race and this race was more important because he might win.

I was allowed to take over; holding Loppy with one hand and lifting the browband of the bridle to squeeze water around his ears. The bottoms of his ears were always sore because they were large and the bridle was small. He lifted his head and nudged me to hurry, his eyes narrowed and trembling from the dribbles. He raised a back foot to show me where another itch was and I crouched to reach the tender stifle within the back leg, smearing the sweat and squeezing a white scum into the bucket, surprised by how much even an abject failure had to give during a hurdle race.

The trainer came to watch me draw the scraper down the dark shine. He didn't speak. He seemed accustomed to anonymous boys. He emptied the bucket and half-filled it at the top, inviting Loppy to drink and slapping his neck with a disdain which seemed cheerful and affectionate. Loppy drank deeply. You could see it going down his throat. He slobbered over the pool at the bottom but the trainer would not give him more; not until he was dry and returned to the London Inn.

At five o'clock, when the last race was being run, we left the racecourse and climbed the long, steep street; towards an inn which was jubilant because both the plated horses had one. The senior lad brought damp bran and Loppy ate it solemnly while the winners fretted, unable to eat, spilling bran from the corners of their mouths, their eyes still wild with the strain of endeavour. I remember wondering about this sport which made people rich and horses old. I'd heard it called the 'Sport of Kings' but it seemed also to be the sport of craftsmen and labourers and swindlers; of hard men who did not care about the horses.

On Friday morning it was over. Horses were led to the railway station and temporary stables were abandoned. At the London Inn, black hens moved in to scavenge the straw and to lay in Loppy's trough. Casual labourers, drafted from the Labour Exchange at ninepence an hour, were sweeping the litter of betting tickets and cartons, those thin green packets which used to hold five cigarettes when five cigarettes cost twopence. They pored over the mess like beachcombers, seeking small silver and coppers, keys and rings for

118

which owners might give rewards. Meanwhile the town went back to work, counting the cost in work at one shilling and threepence an hour; rueful yet not repentant, aware that despite laments about fallen favourites and crooked jockeys, they would respond again next year when the local newspaper announced record entries.

There is no race-meeting in our town now. The fixture was abandoned during the 1939-45 war, considered superfluous to a sport which was becoming increasingly sophisticated and would soon be a popular spectacle on television. What was the racecourse is now put to less spectacular, less social and much more practical uses; but memories are there and Loppy is among them, for ever panting in pursuit like the brave but backward pupil who knows he will never catch up.

# Guides and Articles

## Where Yesterday Leans on the Shoulder of Today

The local guidebook has a humble place in the hierarchy of literature, even the all-inclusive, post-modernist, non-hierarchical hierarchy of today, but an individually written one can be a pleasure to read as well as useful. In 1949 Vian wrote, unacknowledged, the official guide to his home town, perhaps because his mother, now a Labour member of the borough council, was on the publicity association.

The same text was used the following year, and this time he was credited, but only for the sections presented here as 'Totnes for the Moor, the River and the Sea.' It is obvious from the style, however, that he wrote the whole thing. Why this could not be admitted is now an unanswerable mystery. No author for the rest of the text is named, leaving readers to assume either that the words somehow wrote themselves, or were composed collectively by the committee of councillors and bed and breakfast people who made up the association (this seems to be the usual assumption anyway). It is, of course, possible they were written by someone too modest to be named but whose prose style was remarkably like Vian's, even down to the direct recycling of material from his early novels (that phrase about the Guildhall reflecting itself 'like wine in a silver spoon' is a favourite image), but I do not believe this. I offer some extracts here, partly because such writings are so often overlooked, and as an evocative picture of the town as it saw itself sixty years ago. Just don't take the mention of Phoenicians or Brutus too seriously.

120

The Phoenicians came here to barter for the tin mined on Dartmoor; and Danes crept up the river to rob and destroy when South Devon was part of Wessex. Totnes became a burh or fortified town and some of the coins minted here before the Norman Conquest are on view today in the Guildhall. King John granted a charter in 1206, and the honour of Guild Merchant was conferred nine years later. These are facts acknowledged by England. What has to be established is the authenticity of the Brutus Stone.

This stone marks Totnes as an individual, for wherever you hear of the town, you hear of the Brutus Stone. There is a tendency to disbelieve that Brutus, the Trojan, landed at Totnes, but the stone on which he stepped is there in Fore Street, and the story is true as stories go.

Ballads and old histories declare that Brutus landed 'on Totnes Shore,' and 'Totnes Shore' used to reach from Berry Head to Prawle Point. It is quite probable, therefore, that the Trojan explorer's first sight of Britain was that part of the coast known as 'Totnes Shore.'

The town is old, then; two thousand years or more. So let us look at Totnes as it is today; at the gabled houses and narrow pavements, at the long steep street which is at once informal and friendly. Let us look at Totnes as it is that we might find in its shadows and silences a suggestion of what it has been.

The castle stands on the crest of a hill, looking above tumbled roofs to the river and patchwork fields.

Once, however, it looked across marshlands to a river that afforded a natural means of livelihood, but simultaneously presented a perpetual threat, since invaders sailed up the Dart to pillage the district. Before the Norman Conquest and after the Saxons had conquered South Devon, the town was fortified but had no castle.

The Norman baron, Judhel, began to build it in 1067, following the Norman pattern and using Saxon labour. From that time the castle banners flew through peace and war until it ceased to be occupied in the sixteenth century. Discarded then as a shell of no military moment, it crumbled to ruin and determined efforts to preserve it as a monument have been made only recently.

Not as large as one might expect, it is neither inaccessible nor hostile; simply a mellow relic of wars long dead. It is, perhaps, dwarfed by our modern age, yet within it lives a silence accentuated by the hiss of grass and the sighing of the elms.

On the north side of the church of St Mary the Guildhall rests in pools of sunshine and shadow.

Once it was a part of the priory, and the site was granted to the Corporation by King Edward VI. Its old granite pillars were transferred from the Church Walk in 1878, and its canopy forms a shadowed entrance to rooms that have an atmosphere peculiar to themselves; and atmosphere which seems to reflect itself like wine in a silver spoon.

It is a minor museum and offers to the curious such echoes of the past as its stocks and mantraps and Saxon coins. Its doors are open always.

The Council Chamber has a Tudor frieze and the scales of Justice and Equity dated 1624. There are two original proclamations by Oliver Cromwell, and portraits of the mayors of the borough.

Where houses overhang the pavements you find the Butterwalk. Here the 'hose of fine Totnes' was sold when that craft was a local pride. Here farm servants were hired, the husband for the fields, the wife for the kitchen; and on these hiring days the women wore white aprons, the men carried whips. Here also, in quite recent times, women of the farms sold baskets of butter and eggs.

Now the Butterwalk gives to the street a dignity as charming as it is curious.


The church is built of red sandstone; red because of the blood of Jesus Christ...

The Gallows stood on Barracks Hill where the wind blows high...

Harpers Hill is a steep red path which climbs past the Bay Horse Inn. It is part of the old fosseway, and children call it lightly 'old Roman Road.'

Steps Cottage, opposite the Kingsbridge Inn, is not all it seems. The part adjoining the road is not a cottage; the cottage lies behind. Its walls enclose only stone steps which wind up to a small chamber. From this room a window commands what might have been a wide sweep of countryside; and the theory is that Steps Cottage used to be an outlook post for the defence of the borough.

Leechwell is one of the sources of water supply mentioned in the court roll, 1475. There is a fable that once it was called 'Luke's Well' and this change of name can be attributed to a parallel story; that the waters had medicinal qualities, capable of restoring sight, curing rheumatism and the bite of the long cripple (snake). Three troughs are supplied by the same stream, and the water which flows into the centre trough is crystal clear and aching with cold.

You cannot travel around Totnes without being conscious of places that have found immortality in history or the less formal recognition of folklore. You find hamlets so small that they appear to be lost in a valley sunburned with corn, and some of them are of Saxon origin, reached by lanes no less old. Each has a name, intimate and humble; each has a past and a future. Vital hamlets these, apparently slumbering in the afternoon sun, yet industrious, of the soil and fragrant from it, their duty realised, their purposes determined.

# The Customs of the Borough

*The places mentioned above are still recognisable; Vian's descriptions of the town's regatta and carnival are not.*

The oldest municipal custom surviving in Totnes is the annual selection of a mayor, and his or her invitation to office.

The ceremony is not without pageantry, for the newly elected mayor and retiring colleague are accompanied by municipal officers, including the bewigged town clerk, the mace bearer and town crier.

The oath of office is sworn in the Guildhall. It is a public ceremony.

The mayor proclaims the accession to the throne of a new monarch in full regalia, scattering the tidings through the town. It is customary to read the proclamation at the Guildhall, the church and the Brutus Stone, and at the extremities of the borough.

Totnes Regatta is an annual holiday disturbed only by war. It has been revived; indeed, it has been strengthened. The holiday spirit has grown, so that all the town and half its neighbours hug the river banks to watch the water carnival, the swimming, the impromptu deeds of daring, and, of course, the races. This is a gay occasion of much rivalry and good sportsmanship.

Bideford, Exeter, Torquay, Paignton and Dartmouth send crews, contributing to a colourful week when the honour of Totnes is fought for in the water and out of it.

Riders of the district compete at the Gymkhana, while the Totnes and District Show holds a place of honour in Devon. No innovation has been so popular for a long time, and all roads lead to Totnes when the horses are saddled, the dogs brushed, and when the tents are up.

Carnival Week is a feast as old as the hills. It begins with the crowning of the queen, a ceremony performed by the mayor and staged beneath the trees of the Island pleasure park. It continues with dancing, midnight concerts, folk dancing and fancy dress parades. It includes also a cousin of the Helston floral dance, a survival of the days when men and women 'danced out to bring the morning in.'

In the Totnes version, men, women and children dance into all the corners of the town, sometimes passing through houses, often seeking out obscure but historic passages. The dancers are led by the mayor and mayoress, and young and old keep up the traditional pageant of joy.

On the closing day of carnival, in the twilight of the queen's reign, the street procession begins; an occasion of brass bands, and elaborate dresses, nodding plumes and the clatter of hooves. Slowly it rolls down the narrow street, pausing often with bursts of laughter and a jingle of harness, collecting ceaselessly for local charities. It is the climax of the week.

At midnight the queen leaves her throne. Carnival is over. The flags are drawn in, and Totnes goes quietly about its business.

# Through the Lanes to Bow Bridge

Totnes has a secret shared only by those who wander its lanes; and since it is good to wander with a destination, even though that destination be not a primary purpose, let us walk from Totnes to Bow Bridge. At the end of the journey there will be sandwiches by the stepping stones; or perhaps sandwiches and beer. At the beginning there is nothing but strong shoes and an ear for the music overhead.

The lane is Fish Cheaters' lane, a red cleft in the hill. This is the path used by fish hawkers who evaded payment of toll at the toll house on Kingsbridge Hill. You can see the tollhouse through the trees; a little house with vigilant windows. The chowters used to creep down here while the morning was grey and afterwards they used to hawk their fish in Totnes. Everyone knew about the evasion of toll, but nobody did anything about it. Evasion by the use of this lane became a sort of chowters' privilege.

The lane has changed little since those days. It is still enclosed by hedgerows opulent with life.

Listen a moment. There's the thrush, bursting his heart for the joy of day; and there's the cuckoo, his notes falling from nowhere, round and ripe like summer rain. Here is a stream straggling across the lane, polishing its pebbles to the colour of sherry in the sunlight. And there - beneath drooping branches - you see what seems to be woodsmoke, incredibly frail and blue. It is a haze, not of smoke, but of bluebells; thousands that seem to move in a fabulous mist.

We turn left now, still following the chowters' path. Here the bracken is high, and here the hedgerow drops a shoulder so that you can look upon Totnes. It is a view so eloquent that the viewer is inarticulate and the amateur camera dumb; the gleam of a river suddenly shy, the purple of moors and greens of fields. So put your camera away. A view like this is best photographed by the mind.

Beyond the lane there is a second-class road, and beyond that the hill falls to Bow Bridge. A creek potters beneath it, and, where the sun pokes truant fingers through the branches, the water runs

126

swiftly, hurrying from these decorations, this pendant from the sun. It seeks the shadows and dallies there, as dark and warm, as hospitable, as a pint of mild and bitter.

And that reminds me. If you want such hospitality, you can have it. The Waterman's Arms is by the bridge.

# Totnes for Moor, River and Sea

Totnes has Dartmoor at its door.

Throughout the summer chars-a-banc go out daily that you might pass from one world to another; from the modern world to an outlaw kingdom governed by the tors. Thousands make this summer pilgrimage, and from Dartmoor none returns without memories of reckless colours and feckless winds. Wherever you go on the moor - Princetown, Two Bridges or Holne - you will be conscious of the grandeur and of the sleeping strength.

Dartmoor is not a uniform wilderness. Its moods vary, so that while Hay Tor is proud in a tremendous loneliness and Princetown attacked by granite-baffled winds, Widecombe lies among intimate fields. Neither is the moor particularly interested in humanity. It is aloof and preoccupied, having a life of its own. It is greater than mere humans.

Consider a moment the names associated with Dartmoor. Clapper Bridge, Shaugh Prior, Saddle Tor and Blowing House. Names chosen with respect and not a little affection. Consider also the stone walls which trace patterns in a fashion apparently aimless. They were built by craftsmen who are forgotten, as perhaps the craft is forgotten, too. A hefty job it must have been. A worthy one, no less, for a dry stone wall is a delight to the eye and a surprise to those familiar only with bricks and mortar.

Wherever you go on Dartmoor you notice the wind-rough ponies, the random streams, and eccentric bridges. And you will leave with memories of turf that has a magic lilt, and of air that celebrates the day like champagne.

The AA recommends several drives from Totnes to the moor. Selection is difficult. There is no 'best' drive, but you should not miss Hay Tor, Buckland, Blue Waters or Becky Falls.

Widecombe is, of course, too famous to be missed. Its church and yew tree, its forge and fair have been carried in memory or song across the world. You will remember the old song about 'Uncle Tom Cobleigh and all.' Rather remarkable is it that

Widecombe owes a part of its reputation to men who neither lived there nor reached there; for Uncle Tom Cobleigh and his married men set out from Sticklepath to visit Widecombe Fair, and everyone knows what happened to them. Bill Brewer and the rest have survived in folklore wherever the story of Devon is told.

Out of Widecombe the road climbs from a tended valley to barren heights, then falls abruptly to Dartmeet.

The moor does things in a way generous and surprising, and of Dartmeet it has made a show-place, as though all nature had conspired to make perfection of this scene. Trees form a background for the meeting of the waters. Here the young rivers of the moor are united, and, when they continue, they are as one. Devon calls it the River Dart.

Imagine a mellow afternoon with the sun in the river and cotton wool in the sky. Imagine a steamer sleeping by the quay; colourful dresses crowding the decks; nondescript blazers and the inevitable cautious umbrella. Imagine your holiday a moment, and drift down the Dart from Totnes to Dartmouth.

You will not forget this journey, for you are moving past not wooded hills alone, but a host of legends that belong to the river and which are interwoven with and sometimes embellishments of history.

There is the legend of Windwhistle Cottage, haunted these ages, where moonlight listens to the wailing wind; and there is another of silent pools which every year claim a broken heart. There is Anchor Stone, where witches were given to the rising tide, and there are the fantastic tales of scud and storm associated with Raleigh, Davis and Gilbert. All were sons of the river. All took from it their breath of adventure.

This is also a journey into the past, for when the river forgets houses and fields and the things of humanity, it yields itself to the wild stretches. The silence here is high and wide, of the kind almost forgotten in modern England. Here you can see the birds: heron, redshank, curlew and kingfisher. Here you can see the cormorant. It stands erect with wings lifted like a tattered umbrella.

Its reputation is notorious, for each day it consumes its weight in fish. At one time the Dart Fishery Board paid half-a-crown for each one destroyed; but still the cormorant remains, motionless and defiant, pauper of the river.

You pass creeks that hint at mysteries, at hamlets forgotten by rail and by all save the lesser roads. You pass Stoke Gabriel in this way, and that's a pity, because Stoke Gabriel is a village of fishermen and of the tall tales that go with fishermen. Men talk still of the summer of 1921 when hundreds of salmon were caught. Fishin' was fishin' in they days, and, if the old are to be believed, fishermen were fishermen also.

Suddenly you come upon Dittisham, home of the plowman plum. In spring the plum blossoms gives to its trees an April hoar, and in summer the same trees give to you fruit that splutters at your teeth. Dittisham is a village of hills and orchards. The steamer pauses there that you might be sure of this.

Beyond Dittisham the trees billow up the slopes like green smoke, and beyond them there is Dartmouth.

You do not pass Dartmouth. No one passes that friendly town which is considered to be the cradle of the British navy; that zealous town whose soul is stirred by the whisper of the sea. You tarry there to watch the river traffic; to be heckled by gulls; and perhaps to remember that Dartmouth was at one time an apprentice to Totnes; a port and stronghold long before Chaucer.

Throughout history Dartmouth has given its men to the sea, its heart to adventure. Now it rests, as rest it might, its glory not forgotten, its pride not misplaced. It speaks of the days of wooden ships and swashbuckling valour; of booming seas and salt spray flying. It speaks of an age never silent, of an age not always heard. It speaks of England's rise to greatness.


If the moor is at the back door of Totnes, the sea is at its front.

The sea of South Devon is different from the sea of Cornwall. It is tamed. It is not hostile. It is a 'family sea,' especially suited to the young who wish to learn to row or swim, to the experienced who wish to indulge feats of endurance, and to the old, to mother who 'wants a paddle' and to father 'who has not swum for years.' The sea of South Devon is kind to all.

Nowhere is it more kind than it is at Paignton, where the wet sand is cocoa-coloured and seagulls dabble in orphan pools left by the receding tide.

Buses ply all day between Totnes and Paignton, and the journey is short. You take the steep hill out of Totnes and pass the old tollhouse at True Street. Afterwards there is Longcombe, a group of cottages with geraniums in the windows and washing on the line, and after that an avenue of trees guides you to the outskirts of Paignton.

Here all is modern, all spick-and-span in expectation of the 'holiday season.' Cinemas show the newest films, hotels are freshly painted, the grass of the public parks is freshly shaved. At a glance you can see that Paignton is expecting you.

The bus puts you down at the station within two hundred yards of the sea. A few minutes later you are grappling with a deck chair, feeling perhaps very new and rather pale in this unusual environment. It is an environment essentially informal, since there is nothing quite the equal of the beach for removing barriers of social shyness.

So you sit; and half-an-hour later you have graduated to a position of importance. You have found a spade that a boy had mourned as lost; retrieved a ball swiped in your direction by a beach Bradman; and you have thrown a stick for somebody's dog. Now you belong. Now is the time to take off your shoes and squirm your toes in the soft sand. Now is the time to be comfortable.

If you find your pleasures quietly, you need do nothing on Paignton beach. You need only absorb the sun and watch others; the people in the water and the people in boats; the youths who make foam of the shallows; and the children. Particularly the children.

Few seaside resorts have done more for children than has Paignton. Some of the recreations are new, but some are old, as familiar to adults as they are popular with the young. Punch wields his truncheon and leans out to ask questions of faces open-mouthed; the beach artist conjures shapes out of the sand, surrounded by admirers, and, at a respectful distance, by juvenile imitators. There are a dozen diversions of this kind, and you can see them all from your deck chair.

You can be amused without effort. Or you can amuse yourself by setting out on that youthful pursuit of using up as much energy as possible in a short space of time. Either way you acquire in one day a tan not to be found in any place other than South Devon.

Totnes suggests that you spend a day at Paignton or at any of its seaside companions. At Goodrington where the cliff walk is like a red town above the sands; at that summer home of the artist, Brixham; or at Torquay where the sun dances with the sea for partner.

When you return in the cool evening, you will find Totnes old by contrast, leisurely, too, its quietness complementary to your tiredness. Totnes is familiar to you now. You know about it. So it seems that you are coming home.

# The Things that Make Totnes

*It is hard to know just how long Vian supplied the town's official publicity material; the publishers of the guide liked to recycle pictures and text for as long as it was convincingly possible, and dates rarely appear. The following summary of what is clearly a later version of the above guide is quoted in a general introduction to Devon published by the county council in 1957. It is pure Vian, and again uses phrases and descriptions that appear in the early novels. I find it especially poignant that no one would have believed, when he wrote it, that strolling players or beggars were ever likely to be seen again on the streets of Totnes.*

*Hamilton-Leggett's* Dartmoor Bibliography *also lists Vian as the 'editor' of the* Official Guide to Bovey Tracey *c1965, but I have yet to come across this.*

Brutus, the Trojan, came here before Britain was Britain, or disciplined time began – there is the stone as proof. William, the Conqueror, came in 1067 and knights went from its castle to the Crusades. Now the castle is a shell, haunted by banners and bugles, guarded by sighing elms.

An arch carves its shadow across the street. Beneath it you will feel yesterday to be reawakened, see the cavalcade that passes through its gate, merchant and beggar and strolling player. On your right steps ascend to Ramparts Walk, and if you pass along it you will find granite pillars and autumnal colours, winking casements and polished cobbles. You will find the Guildhall: it kneels in the sun, its glory in timbers as fine as old wine. The church is red. In its screen lives the craftsmanship of the fifteenth century – a torrent of beauty, humanity's music in stone. Here is artistry, work hallowed by purpose.

The Butterwalk belongs to a colourful age – an age of coaches and horses, bonnets and buckles, and beer at a penny a pint. The Butterwalk knows all about it: its echoes will tell you the tale.

These lanes are yours, they give you red earth for a carpet and branches for a roof of sighs. They lead to surprises: a cottage with its thatch out-at-the-elbows like an old coat; a stile with initials deep in its heart; or a hill from which you can see tumbled roofs and quiet spires; fields bleeding from the plough, and others that are young and green. On the opposite hill there is a conference of trees and, away in the haze, Dartmoor.

The mood of the river is an evening mood. Here trees come down from the hills and stoop to see themselves as others see them; here skiffs dawdle; and here the river smiles to show where trout have been. When the sky closes over like the healing of a wound the noises of the river come out from their hiding places and you can hear them plainly - the sounds of moor-hen, peal and trout - sudden sounds made loud by the calm all round.

These things make Totnes – Guildhall, arch, church, Butterwalk and castle; lanes and meadows and river. These things *are* Totnes, peace and maturity through endeavour. When you have come you will know; until you have come none can tell you. For the story of Totnes is not in words, only in itself.

# Dittisham – The Beachcomber Village

*From the river boats, in the summer, you can get the impression that Dittisham is no more than a celebrity estate of million-pound homes. In fact, as I found when I was last there, on a cold winter Sunday afternoon, it is a varied and lively community, and Vian would feel at home in both the Red Lion and the Ferry Boat (in one of which I actually met a man who remembered him). Still, a lot of things have changed since he lived there and wrote this colourful portrait of it. Published as 'Dittisham Pocket Souvenir - newly written by Vian C. Smith' in 1949, it is less restrained than his Totnes one; he obviously did not feel the committee leaning over his shoulder in the village as he did in the town.*

*This is the sort of guide with 'researched in the pub' stamped all over it (not a criticism – I have written a few like that myself). Everything concerning Sir Walter Raleigh, for instance, is completely wrong: Raleigh Country is in East Devon, where the hero was born and grew up, and any connection with Dittisham is minimal. The rather lugubrious humour about getting the donkey into the ferry, and the dated bar-room sexism of the Anchor Stone story, are actually quite untypical of Vian, and my first instinct was to cut them out, but I decided to leave them; he was as complex and contradictory as the rest of us, and it is no use pretending otherwise. He always hated any ill treatment of animals, and his empathy for women, and deep understanding of their real lack of equality, are apparent throughout his work, not least the novels he was writing at this time.*

*The point of the Sammy Coombes story is that he was severely physically disabled, and his skills as a boatman were deemed almost miraculous as a result, making him famous far beyond the Dart. Vian also omits to say that Coombes was known as a singer, his favourite song being the one where a man leaves a live crab in the chamber pot without telling his wife; when she gets up to use it, the crab attaches itself to her in a most Rabelaisian manner. They used to regularly fall about in the Ferry Boat Inn at that one.*

*What comes across most clearly is Vian's real engagement with the life of the village. There is no feeling of the aloof, isolated artist looking down, but of a man living in a community and enjoying the opportunity to celebrate it.*

Dittisham sits on the river wall, its feet in the water, its trousers rolled for the brown sun. It dawdles in a calm akin to the mood of the river; a beachcomber village, equally colourful, with the philosophy of the beachcomber and the attendant conviction that it has no philosophy at all.

Of its age Dittisham is not sure. It murmurs vaguely of the tenth century, hints at an infancy Saxon, at a youth startled by the Norman Conquest. That the church prayed on the hill in 1050 is true enough. It is the earliest date the old beachcomber can remember.

It prefers to talk not of dates, but of people; of Gilbert, Davis and Raleigh who lived their boyhood on the river, and who caught the insinuating, the adventurous smell of the sea.

Humphrey Gilbert was born on the site of what is now Greenway House. In the reign of Elizabeth, when England turned its face to the salt winds, he set out for Newfoundland in *The Golden Hind*, a ship of forty tons. The ship was lost, its explorer also, but a page of history was won.

Davis too heard the crying of the gulls, and left the river for scud and storm. He ventured northwest of Greenland, discovering the straits which honour his name. But neither haunts Dittisham as does Raleigh.

More than a name, Raleigh is a word. It says all that England is, and, through mastery of the seas, has been. Here he was born, here he smoked that pipe of tobacco, here his name is whispered by trees and tides, chucked about by boatmen with the negligence of familiarity. This is Raleigh country.

Dittisham used to have its donkey; a tireless animal, humble enough to be willing, his farthing hooves picking penny sounds out of cobbles.

The village drove its donkey to market, but, when the river had to be crossed, donkey became passenger, and took time off to think things over. To persuade him into the boat needed patience and good fortune. Fore legs in was an achievement, yet only a beginning.

Rear must follow, sooner or later. And when it was later the interval held its breath.

This ceremony was performed in various manners. Some pulled, some pushed, some made wooing noises. Whatever the way, it was a free show. One man made a habit of picking up his donkey, and sitting it in the stern where it could meditate in comfort. He was the sort of fellow who would be a success in any community and in any age.

The first vehicle ferry simplified matters, for a drop prow enabled the donkey to embark without loss of dignity. A second and improved ferry made the whole business so simple as to be commonplace. The element of chance was reduced to a minimum. To be or not to be was no longer the question. Ceremony ceased. Security had arrived. It was a sign of the times.

Quietly the village donkey died, to be buried politely in a field near the rectory. The Austin Seven took its place, and the car ferry appeared. It marked the passing of an age all chance and strong language for another swift and lubricated, neat enough to be featureless.

The fun has gone. Any driver can manoeuvre a car from slip to ferry. To manipulate a donkey was a different matter.

When ships were swans and canvas sighed for wind, Dittisham rolled up its sleeves for the export of iron ore. Ships came to Dartmouth with coal, and loaded iron ore instead of ballast. Barges were poled up and down the river. The ore, mined near Dittisham, was brought to the quay by donkey pannier. And as a result of this trade, Dittisham thrived.

Inevitable result of prosperity, pubs thrived also, their dignity preserved by the name of 'inn.' There were seven, including two cider houses, and all were small, informal enough to be friendly. They helped to satisfy a prodigious thirst.

The introduction of steam, and the development of vessels in no need of ballast, knifed this trade, and reduced the mines to shells. Barges slept, lights went out in five of the seven inns, and Dittisham went back to fishing.

As a fishing village, it has never let the Dart get away with much. It can tell of silver harvests, or of nights when the river scowled in grudging mood. It can tell of the time a school of bass came in with the dawn; or of how a crew dipped eight hours solid, tons of sprats to be sold at a florin a barrel; and of the night when the Dart, weary of parsimony, gave up its salmon in a gesture as impulsive as it was embarrassing. It can tell of the biggest salmon, the biggest lobster. It can tell of the best boat, the best crew, the best season. It can tell anything you might want to hear.

But the chances are it will not tell the same story twice.

Women carried baskets to Paignton and Torquay. The produce varied with the seasons. Snowdrops, daffodils, water cress, primroses, lent lilies, mussels, cockles, pears, apples, and, lastly, when mornings hissed with autumn rain, mushrooms of proud and perfect shape.

These women hawked the fruits of minor harvest, then walked home in darkness or in the cathedral calm of summer evening. That was before the donkey, even before the hand-cart. It was when work was hard and wrists were strong.

Each season meant more pennies for purses thin and families large. But the greatest of all seasons was the plum. It is still.

It's a busy season, as new and as bountiful as summer seems always to be. It's a brief season, and, at the end of each day, there's beer on the step and the chance for talk. Dittisham lives in its orchard, then, hand picking dessert fruit to save the bloom, or shaking a hail of damsons into sheets spread on the grass. It's a business for the family.

There are three kinds of plum. Two are damson types, called, for the want of names, 'small reds, small blacks.' These make fine jam. Devonshire women say no jam can compare with it. Each is a kitchen plum, delighting the cook who has been harassed by shortages or substitutes.

Then there is the plowman, pride of the village, a dessert fruit that has dragged down branches and brought bounty out of withered winter.

About the plowman there is a secret.

Attempts have been made, and are being made, to grow the plowman in other parts of the country. Hitherto these attempts have failed. Probably they will fail again, for even across river at Greenway the plowman tree refuses to prosper.

Yet experiments continue in the county and elsewhere. Men spend small fortunes in labour and patience trying to nurse a plowman tree into growth, and, after growth, to the production of healthy fruit. They are willing to go on trying in the belief that success will justify all. Such persistence is a comment on humanity's refusal to accept the inevitable as much as a tribute to the plum.

So far none has satisfactorily emulated what Dittisham has done negligently and by accident.

Many theories have been advanced as to how and when and by whom the plowman was introduced to a village hitherto renowned for its damson types. Some of these stories are extravagant and beautiful, implausible enough to be readily believed, but the most probable is so simple that it is in danger of being dismissed as unworthy of such a tree.

About eighty years ago, Jack Gilding, a merchant seaman whose home was in Dittisham, returned from the continent with a tree. Or perhaps it was more than one tree. Perhaps it was a dozen. No matter. The important fact is that he returned from the continent, and the German word for plum tree is 'pflaumen-baum.' A pretty fair pronunciation of 'pflaumen' is 'plowman.' So there is good reason to suppose that the proud plum is of German origin, although why it has flourished here and not elsewhere in England remains a mystery.

It is a fruit fat with goodness. It splashes at your teeth. It is also a fluke. So make the most of it while you may.

Half of Dittisham is legend, and why not? Where there is no recorded history the soil is fertile with lore.

There is the fable of the Dart; every year the river claims a human heart; and there are the rival legends about the purpose of Anchor Stone.

Some say the Anchor Stone was the rock where witches were chained that they might see the peering tide. If this is true, perhaps the village came out to watch the struggle and to hear the cries. Perhaps the river sneered as it rose; slowly, of course, because that was essential. And perhaps it made no sound as it swallowed the woman and swelled above her.

Others say no, not a place for witches, but a ducking stool for shrews. It is not common knowledge that there were shrews before, say, the fashion for slimming, but, if the story is true, there must have been; however temporarily. A wife who lived before her time, who anticipated criticism as a feminine prerogative, and received her ever-loving with something more concrete than affection, did not have the last word. By some devise that does, alas, elude the imagination of the twentieth century, she was appended to this stone and left to reflect.

Ultimately she was released when tide and tears were about to mingle.

It seems that the threat or use of this ducking stool maintained a high level of domestic discipline. Obviously times have changed, women with them. I don't suppose men have changed. We have merely lost hope of having the last word.

The village regatta is not dead. It lives in discussion wherever river men congregate to smoke and sup and swap.

It was an alfresco affair, chiefly remarkable for its accidents. None forgets the time the starter's gun went off, the trousers of a committee man with it.

Boats came and went, *The Mite* and *Superb* among them, but the most famous of all was *The Black Plum*. A fishing boat, light with yellow pine, it won all honours on the river. About it there is a story.

*The Black Plum* had been cock-of-the-walk a long time, taking on all-comers with a generosity contemptuous. Its supremacy was challenged by *The Veronica*, a sleek and varnished craft; the match was fixed; and half the district turned out to watch. The boats lined up, one manicured like a mannequin, the other broad and stout, a Devon matron. Crews exchanged familiarities the way crews do. At the third attempt the gun went off.

Of a measured two miles, the second mile was against the tide. Steadily *Veronica* drew away. She had a comfortable lead at the turn, and her supporters began to cheer her home. Then Sammy Coombes took a hand.

Coxswain of *The Black Plum*, he sacrificed lengths for the ebb tide. River magic swept his boat into a lead as effortless as it was miraculous. It was all over bar the shouting, and the shouting lasted a long time.

As a story it is Sammy Coombes' triumph.

How does Dittisham spend its leisure? That is a question asked by many who are accustomed to Odeons and Empires, to trams every minute and Saturday night in the gods. The answer depends on the time of year.

In spring there are daffodils hob-nobbing in the orchards, primroses spilling cream over the hedgerows. These are gathered, arranged in bunches, twelve to a bunch or thirteen for luck; and baskets overflowing with spring are carried into towns where flowers are niggardly or corporation property.

Summer means work for all, even if it's only erecting the barbed wire that invites heifers to inspect the cricket pitch. Boats sleep on the river, awaiting the accident of salmon; fly fishermen hunt stickle water; and farm workers clump down from the fields, their shirts red with earth, their hair bleached by the sun. Those who find leisure in idleness can watch the grass come and go with sheen, or hear the murmur of bees plotting with the summer air. And those who are young need suffer no hardship, for they have the hay to be young in.

At what point summer becomes autumn none is sure. It varies with the seasons, and, in the event of an Indian summer, is postponed until October. Then, of course, it is pushed against winter and doesn't survive. But, no matter what date it moves in, it brings out the lurchers on Sunday mornings, and fills the pot at Sunday noon. Football returns, a man short where cricket left off. There are games on the hill on Saturday afternoons, and excuses in the pub afterwards.

Then there's winter. Winter's different. There are concerts and carols, whist drives and dances. There's something for everyone. Even Johnny Allen. He spends his winter trying to get double one.

A whist drive is advertised. It will be held in the schoolroom at 7.30. Notices have been printed by patient crayons and distributed to the shops. They kneel in the windows.

At seven o'clock a light opens its eye in the schoolroom. Iron screams on wood as desks are arranged in rows, the tops making tables. In no time the room is ready. It has ceased to be the place where junior scholars are told to do it again. It has become the hall of chance, where all depends on the cut for trumps.

People arrive in groups, so many shillings for the fund. The secretary becomes master of ceremonies, ringing a bell to prove it. Players sit, despite the junior benches. Thumbed cards go the rounds, so accustomed to the game that they need no guidance. They play without heart. Long ago they gave up hope of ever affording satisfaction.

The first trump appears. Fortunes are established. Partners blunder. The interval allows time for a cup of tea or a pint. Over either you can explain why you refused to yield your ace. You can do this safely, because no one will listen.

A bell rings. The M.C. loves the noise, and sends it on wings to the pub across the road. Play resumes, excitement mounts for some and expires for others. Faces are shining or blank. The last trump is played. It goes down with a bang, as befits the last trump.

Ownership of the cut-glass dish is established. Somebody has had a good evening.

Once a year Dittisham has its Horticultural Show. It sits in the middle of summer like a broody hen, hatching a hundred pounds for charities. It sleeps through May and June, but late July it wakes with a squawk, and the village needs a week to recover.

As a show it is not more remarkable than are others of its kind. That is to say it is remarkable.

Many qualities combine to make it so. Everyone says 'Going to the show?' and everyone answers 'No.' It's a good sign. Everyone goes. None confesses his intention to exhibit, but entries are palmed to the secretary in good numbers, albeit two days later than the advertised date of closing. This subterfuge is essential, for without secrecy a horticultural show would be nothing.

Cottage gardens become eloquent, to be assessed by phrases such as 'first prize,' 'third prize' and 'highly commended.' X, in his casual Sunday stroll, chances to glance over the wall and note the welfare of Y's beans. The children of Z climb the wall so that they can tell dad about them. And later Y is dismayed to hear that his beans 'Be proper, best ever did see, no sense showin' against 'em.' Y is angry. Such information will reduce entries in his class, even perhaps give him a walkover. It will reduce triumph to nothing more than seven and sixpence.

The day arrives. Tents stand on one leg, hesitate, and spread their skirts. Produce comes in, and the horticultural tent is serious with smells. Each exhibit is judged twice. Once in the morning, once in the bar.

It's better fun the second time. It lasts longer.

The population of Dittisham is approximately five hundred.

When cattle were sent across river to market, a 'pound' stood where 'The Cabin' is now. Animals were retained there until claimed by their owners.

The churchyard of St George's Church has been in use since 1198. Eighteen thousand persons have been buried there.

American troops carried out a friendly occupation during the war. Every cottage had its friend: Elmer from the Middle West, or perhaps it was Bill from Brooklyn. When the invasion of France was imminent, crafts of all kinds snored in the river, awaiting the order which would send these soldiers of the new world to assist in the reprieve of the old. One morning the village woke up to find the river empty. The invasion of France was on.

The *Magna Britannia* shows that the villages in the parish in 1822 were Higher Dittisham, Dittisham Wales and Capton.

Dittisham used to sell its wife.

The last recorded sale was in the middle of the nineteenth century, when a husband, inspired by the highest motives, sold his wife to a bachelor old enough to know better. Money changed hands. The deal was completed. So she returned to her lawful husband the next day.

# Talk Which Knows its Home

Once upon a time, when blossom blushed new like the bride, I walked a fat and leaning lane towards the cottage in the valley; there to spend mild days with friends who were old in years as well as affection and who would welcome me with the kind of quiet which belongs to the country like sunshine to the trees.

And as I walked, I remembered some of the words which the old couple used; all spoken unaware from some secret fund, each a dialect word inherited from other generations and graced with that flair for description which is the surprise of good Westcountry talk.

I remembered how the old man said: 'Guzberries be adaggin,' mother, us better get'm in.' The word describes the bush; so round-shouldered with abundance that the fruit is adaggin' (dragging) near the cold and sun-forgotten earth.

It was his wife who taught me that beautiful phrase, 'light's vanity;' using it twice, once in approval of pastry, then in amusement when friend George went homeward with the cider blinking in him. 'There goes George, steppin' it out downalong, light's vanity.' George was, too, for cider is like love and lets you walk on air.

Gardeners speak with disparagement of their wives picking flowers and fruit or finger-thumbing what might be a weed and is probably artichoke or horse-radish. Spuddlin' is the word for it. 'Tis mother bin yer spuddlin.' I told her about it times.' It's the word which mother returns when she says of father, 'He's out the back, spuddlin' about doin' nort.' It's a harmless word, spoken with mock reproach like the play of dogs in a meadow. You are not meant to believe it, nor interpret it as idle or lazy or similar country sins.

Beautiful birds should have names that sing, which is why the yellow-hammer becomes the 'golden gladdy.' Then there's the eccentric, mildly comic 'tidley-tops' for wren; meaning perhaps small head. There is 'postis-legs' for robin, a comment on that prize-fighter's thin and fragile legs; for to be as thin as a post is to be thin indeed. There's the improbable 'eckimile' for the peck-a-minute, watch-a-second blue tit, while the sleep of sunshine is in the 'wooin' bird,' dialect for pigeon.

As I walked this lane in the once upon a time, I thought of the poetry which smiles in our dialect like mischief in the eye; and I thought this poetry is neglected or denied because there are fashions in language, as in all else, and the fashion is to deride talk which knows its home. But it is no mean talk which can make 'cockleet' of cock's light, then use it for dawn. It is no thin language which finds 'dimpsey' for twilight, 'Lent lily' for daffodil, then kneels among the 'goocoos' when they drift like woodsmoke across the secret earth. The countryman calls the bluebell 'goocoo' without knowing or caring the origin of the name, except that 'Gran alwis called'm that. Said it times her used to. The goocoos be ablawin'. I minds her sayin' that.'

I remembered how the country gift is received shyly, then 'jewelled safe' for ever. How the hedgerow hen 'staules her eggs' by laying them in some place of jealous hoard. How the countrywoman pampers her 'guzen-chicks' (goslings), and how the dusty dog 'ketches round twice' before settling himself to sleep.

Remembering all this I came to the cottage in the valley; where the cat called the sun its own and the garden yawned in the heat. The kitchen was dark with happy reflections, like wine when you show it light; so there we sat in the stone-paved cool, while clock 'knacked' the hour, and mother 'scawved' together the memory of a fire. 'Scawve' is a word remembered from the stoop of harvest; when women followed the cutting blades, their wooden rakes 'scawvin' in the corn.

I remember how in the evening of that day, when there was no haste in the world nor harassment nor fear, I went out to the garden with the old proud man and let him tell me about his flowers, each leaning down, holding its sunshine to console the night. He needed no answers, only one to listen, and as he moved like a priest among known children, I felt the come-around of evening.

Twilight came in the gate, quiet of skirt and tall and scented. Evensong sang in the grass, and fat hens settled to their brown and puffed out warmth. We stayed until the stars were pale, until the country darkness was darkest in the trees. Then slowly we went indoors; to the kitchen where mother sat beside the kettle, and the 'long-sleeve' clock said supper.

We had supper there, while the old man told how the 'worried' be good for gardens; meaning seaweed and calling it oarweed, then corrupting it. They told of brother John who was a 'nellier' (slater); of their friend who played the 'melodeon' (concertina); and of how bedtime comes when tiredness says that there can't be 'two forenoons in one day.'

Then slowly and gradually we went to bed; 'up the wooden hill' said mother. Candlelight wagged on the landing, and in the bed there was a water bottle. 'Wan of the stone sort, just to take the frug (chill) from the sheets.'

We each said 'Good-night' several times. Then mother said 'See ee bim'bye,' meaning in the morning; and the old man said, 'Proper day t've bin, proper masterpiece.'

With this lovely dialect word the candles moved away, taking their shadow and leaving me with mine. It was big on the ceiling and stooping, like a hunchback. It was a stranger so I blew it out and went to the window and leaned there, listening to the garden and the cool and gentle night.

GC

# Silent Birth in the Dark Night

It's the oldest light in the world. It's the light of the shepherd going to tend his sheep. A hundred years ago the light was a lantern, the candle living precariously within transparent horn. Then came the hurricane lamp, its wicks burning with dandelion colours, its paraffin making slopping sounds. Trimming the wicks was a job for the wife.

Now the light is a torch, a big white eye, as vigilant as a searchlight probing for trouble during the war. But looking after it is still the wife's job.

She must check battery, bulb, switch. She must also see that in his pockets he has string, brandy, his knife with the thin blade curved like a seagull's beak. As she follows him to the door, she makes certain of something else; that beneath his old, long coat he has sacks wrapped around his body, one in front like an apron, the other behind, both tied with yellow cord. The sacks keep him warm. They thicken his tall, frugal frame.

She watches the light move away. The dog goes too, its vest showing white, the rest of its body darker than the dark. She closes the door, keeping in the warmth, which might be all-important soon.

She builds the fire with logs; there's milk on the stove, in readiness. She watches the clock, wondering how long it will take him.

The eyes of the sheep are reflected in his torch. They wait for him to spot the first signs. A ewe on her own; that's one of the signs, because the instinct for privacy is strong. A ewe turning in fretful circles, like a dog trying to lie down; that's another.

He does not interfere. Birth is what spring is all about. Healthy ewes are not alarmed or weakened, and strong lambs are soon safe,

147

but he needs to be here; to be assured that all is well; to give help quickly when it isn't.

He is looking for twins. About thirty percent of lambs are twins and the danger is that even when delivery is normal, the ewe will fuss one and neglect the other. Usually the firstborn is her favourite. The other will be left to shiver. It's then that the shepherd persuades her to accept the second, to identify its smell and acknowledge responsibility. If she is stubborn, he takes both lambs to the barn. The ewe follows, her face looking up, freckled with worry.

He closes the door to confine them, and in the dark hours she becomes adjusted to the idea of two. By dawn the second is as important as the first; the ewe swanks out to show the morning what a wonderful thing happened in the night.

Triplets and quads make pretty photographs, but the shepherd knows they are too many. One is always weak; vulnerable to the enemies in the sky or to the menace in the undergrowth.

The enemies in the sky are crows, rooks, seagulls. They pounce at dawn, challenging the ewe to leave the strong to protect the weak. Sensibly she does not. She stands over the strong and stares defiance, and the birds destroy the weakling.

The menace in the undergrowth is the fox. It is swift and clever. The shepherd hates it, yet his hatred is complicated by respect for its brains, its readiness to take risks to provide for its own.

He points his torch beyond the sheep to the undergrowth, listening for a fox and watching the dog, trusting the dog to hear it or smell it. The dog understands. It is still with listening. For a while suspicions become apprehensions, and the dark is alive with shadows.

One of the ewes has triplets and one of the lambs is weak. The shepherd crouches over it, coming between it and the cold while he gropes in a pocket for the bottle. 'Aspirins' says the label, although it's years since it contained aspirins.

He moistens the lamb's mouth with brandy, then reaches beneath his coat for one of the sacks.

He wraps the lamb in the sack and carries it through the dark to the warm oblong of the kitchen window. His wife hears his boots and has the door open. No word passes between them. She knows what to do.

She carries the lamb to the hearth and places it on the sack. Then she covers it with an old coat, bought years ago, or perhaps inherited, kept hanging in the passage against such an emergency.

She tips warm milk in a saucer and dips her little finger. She puts the finger in a corner of the lamb's mouth, cradling up its head so it can swallow. The milk dribbles down her wrist. She wastes most of it. She dips again and persuades again; the lamb begins to respond.

Her face is quiet in the firelight while she saves the lamb. She does not talk about it, cannot find words for it, but in her tiredness she knows she is not only saving something which might be worth five pounds later on. She is saving life; that precious spark which is always new.

In the morning the shepherd brings the fleece of a lamb which died in the night. He fits the fleece over the back of the lamb which his wife has saved, doing it neatly to deceive.

He carries the lamb from the kitchen to the yard, showing it to the bereaved ewe. She almost welcomes it, then becomes suspicious. She breathes her nostrils over its head and rejects it. She thinks again and breathes her nostrils along its back. She is confused. She smells the back again and is convinced. She accepts the lamb as hers and nudges it towards the milk.

The shepherd glances to his wife. Again no word is spoken. She remains in the yard, making sure the ewe's suspicions do not come back. He hurries to the tractor. Its trailer is loaded with mangolds.

He drives through frosted mud, scattering good food so the ewes can supply their young. Not until the lambs are ten days old will they begin to tear snatches of grass; not for twelve weeks will they be wholly independent. Meanwhile the shepherd will bring hay, mangolds, swedes, nursing them like nursing a multitude, watching the weather.

His wife sees what it does to him; he is as tough as hawthorn, but every lambing season is a year tireder. She brings steaming tea to his chair beside the fire, watching the firelight drug his face until he is giving in to tiredness like giving in to drowning.

There are more sheep in Devon than in any other county. Last year the figure was over a million. This is not only because of the mild climate and early grass. It is partly because of tradition. Devon makes sheep-men as Ireland makes horse-men. The wife knows this. Her husband is part of this tradition. She also sees his face in sleep and knows what it costs in time and worry and working in the night.

The dog looks up, feeling her concern and sharing it. For a moment they are united in devotion. The dog shifts slightly until it is lying across his feet. The wife puts more logs on the fire. Instinctively they are warming him, bringing him comfort as he brought the mercy of warmth to young life lying in the dark.

WR

# How it all Begins in the Cold Fields

The silence is cold on the hill. Only the bare field and trees as thin as scribbles. Only a greyness that burns your face and makes your breath like smoke. It is an afternoon in January. The countryside seems dead.

Then a sound grumbles into the quiet. A tractor climbs from the farm, its wheels breaking the cold crust of the lanes and churning up the mud. It struggles into the field and trails its load. It is spreading dung.

Before the war this job was done by horse and cart. The horse was slow and seldom shod. Its feet were peasant poor. The cart had heavy wheels, crusted with mud. Its iron chains made blinking sounds. The man had a sack around his shoulders, sometimes another around his waist. His face was thin with cold, his hands were all bone.

For days on end his work began in the yard, where he forked the manure from heap to cart, using a long-handled 'prang' or 'evil,' and throwing with a long, lean rhythm. Then up the hill to the fields, where he scattered the dung and called it 'muck,' denigrating it in the process.

Muck-spreading was never something the romanticists wrote about or press photographers came to photograph. But for me it always represented the part of agriculture which the townsman seldom sees. Weekend cars might stop to admire the corn. They do not realise how it all begins.

Nothing much has altered in thirty years, except that some farms have less stock, making muck even more precious if they are not to rely entirely on artificial substitutes. Now it is almost all cow dung, for dairy herds have been increased. Horse dung is comparatively rare. It is sold to amateurs for their roses or to professionals who grow mushrooms.

Another change is the tractor, succeeding the horse; while trailer or muck-spreader has succeeded the stiff old cart. But the man's the same. He has waterproof clothing instead of sacks, but he seems to be wearing the same cap. The loneliness is the same, too, perhaps even greater since he has no horse to hear his swearing. The cold is enough to make anyone swear.

Those central-heated journalists who write glibly of the need to increase productivity; those plumb economists who complain that the working man does not work hard enough; they ought to be here on this January hill, with the sky low enough to touch.

After the spreading comes the ploughing, turning the earth to rain and frost. Frost is the farmer's friend. It breaks the earth. The best frosts break it 'as fine as gunpowder,' so that to harrow it twice is to have it ready for drilling.

Drilling wheat and barley is a serious business hereabouts. Watching the corn come green in the mellow weather of May and June is one of the excitements of being alive in a countryside which is always striving. By July even the townsman will see that magic has touched the fields and filled them with bounty. In August the quality of the harvest will become national news. Holiday cameras will snatch photographs of sun-drenched men in the cornfields. There will be ritualistic sighs for the good old days when horses drew the reaper.

But August is eight months away. The process is beginning now with the lonely work on the hill.

It is being done by men chronically underrated, so underpaid that other trades unions would be insulted. We overrate mediocre talents and pay through the nose for entertainers. If you want to be somebody in this world you do not grow the food which society needs for survival. You learn three chords on a guitar. When will we grow up?

MDA

# Bringing the Hay to the Lofts

There is a trundling sound in the sunshine lane. So you call back your dog and wait for whatever it is to turn the corner.

They are bringing in the hay. The trailer is top-heavy and the bales are bulging and the farmer's son who drives the tractor has been burned the colour of teak.

They are bringing the hay to the lofts, where it will remain for about six months; until winter has shrivelled the grass and bullocks stand at the gate, waiting for their winter ration.

The hay is loaded with sunshine. It smells sweet. The smell is as tantalising as the smell of bread from a country bakehouse. It drones in the yard as men and boys throw the bales to the loft. It is a smell which those boys will never forget. When they are old, they will catch a breath of it and be immediately cast back, as I am cast back, to those summers which seem in memory to have been always sunshine.

My memory goes back to men long dead, to bearded men, tall and thin and tough; to horses nodding off the flies; to women coming through the gate with baskets, big, country baskets, covered with white cloths. Those women wore sun-bonnets tied beneath their chins. Their skirts were long. They brought the men's tea. And tea in the hayfield was always one of the sweetest meals of the year.

I remember the cucumber and jam, the cold meats, the home-baked bread with crusts that crackled. The women poured hot tea from big jugs and the tea brought the sweat trickling down. The men were served first. Then the youths, then the younger boys. You had to wait your turn in those days. My hair itches as I remember the heat, the dust, the scratch of the hay when you sprawled in it and looked up to the sky. My eyes narrow as I remember the way the turned grass shone.

Mowing machines and rakes were drawn by horses and during the break for tea, the horses were led to the shade of trees. They were oppressed by heat, worried ragged by flies. The flies of the July field are big and fat and persistent. They freckled the faces of the horses and gathered in clusters around the eyes. When I was so small that I had to reach upward, making a long arm and tiptoeing for the biggest horse, I spent the tea break waving flies from the horses' faces and hoping that someone would save me a sandwich. Preferably cucumber. Although usually it was cheese.

The horses and the flies and the smell of hay; they are part of my childhood. Only a child knows how to hate and I hated those flies and the black sound they made.

This week I heard it again as they clamoured around my own horses, biting tears from the corners of their eyes. This week I hated them just as viciously, swatting blows at them with a disgust which tool me back forty years to the days of harness bells and feed bags and tails ticking regularly like a clock.

It has been a good harvest; better than good in some places. One farmer told me that in his twenty years it is the best ever crop. Another, rather older and perhaps more difficult to please, said that long sunshine alone does not guarantee good hay. 'Good weather makes bad hay,' is an old-time maxim. It is based on the assumption that a farmer tends to rush the cutting and drying and baling, fearful that the weather is too good to last. Erratic weather compels him to give his hay time. That at any rate is the theory. My own observation is that any farmer who is not pleased to get his hay safely in 'must be mortal hard to satisfy.'

There is always a sense of jubilation as the last load comes trundling through the lane. It's been a gruelling period, since the routine tasks of a farm do not stand still to allow time for hay-making. For two weeks or more the farmer and his sons and labourers have been working from cock-light to dusk, without time to read of debates in Parliament or threats of crisis or strikes in other industries. They have brought the first half of summer safely home. Now the corn is ripening and the second half is near.

It won't be long before the experienced farmer, leaning on his gate, will hear the crackling sound which barley makes when it is ready. Then

154

it will be from cock-light to dusk again, with casual labour called up like reservists at a time of crisis. Men will slog the sun down while Fleet Street leader writers, no less crackpots for having millions of readers, will perpetuate the legend that in the 1960s men have forgotten how to work.

*MDA*

# Sketches, Memories and Opinions

# Family Affair

The afternoon was white and still; like a bowl of milk. The sun made hot shadows, and one of these shadows moved.

The cat moved with purpose, her head low, her tail erect. She moved out of the yard towards the house. She looked at the house, at the windows which answered like eyes; and the windows confided what she wished to know. The old man was asleep.

She passed out of stunned sunshine to the half-light of the porch; and there she paused, tense with watchfulness, her tail down, her eyes bright. She watched the long brown dog, and the long brown dog knew she was there and kept both eyes shut determinedly. The cat knew he was afraid.

She flicked her tail once, then moved around him; moving delicately, with a derision precise.

The light in the kitchen was brown, like sunlight in a stream. She waited, listening to the silence upstairs. She knew what would happen if the old man found her there. Then she looked to the opened door of the scullery; where a woman worked.

The woman was grey and strong, and the smells she made were the hot sweet smells of jam. The cat saw the bowl, the wooden spoon; the empty jars which changed red when she poured. The cat waited, for she knew the risks.

The woman turned and saw the cat. A moment there was alarm in her eyes. Then she remembered the silence upstairs and said, 'You shouldn't be in.' But she said it in a hushed way, like a conspiracy, and the cat knew she could come forward now.

157

The woman found a saucer and poured milk. She put the saucer deep beneath the sink, among the scrubbing brushes and fat brown cloths. Then she stood at the sink so that her legs and skirt and apron concealed the low, black crouch. The lapping tongue made little ticking sounds, so she pushed a tap to drown them. It drowned her voice when she said, 'There's been no rain. Of course you want a drink.'

The cat turned from the empty saucer, flicking a foot. She went out with dignity, and the long brown dog let her pass. Only when he was sure it was too late did he raise his head in elaborate indignation and dart a pretence of pursuit.

The cat turned and looked at him. The long brown dog stopped, wanting to bark, to tell somebody about this, this conspiracy of milk, but the long brown dog knew better; for the old man was asleep. So he shrugged as though it didn't matter, as though he were too hot, too tired. Then he went back to his curled-up place in the porch.

The cat moved on; down the path and through the yard; around the litter of firewood and wire-netting and broken chicken coops, then upward to the loft. The steps were broken and full of ferns. At the top was a door, crusted on its irons. Two of its boards were broken, and the hole was her way in.

She passed into the gloom and the smells of hay. She went around the bales, in and out like a maze; hurrying deeper and deeper into her secret, hurrying faster and faster because now she was alone with her secret and could show her fear. She was afraid for her young.

They were hidden where the floor faltered on a broken beam; where no great boot dared tread. She stood a long moment, looking back and listening; listening to the sunshine. Then she came to them and licked them, comforting their heads, promising their blindness. She lay down and stretched; giving herself to their greed. In her eyes was the shine of deep content.

GC

# Orchard Hour

She stood in the green world and called her hens. 'Cooop, cooop, cooop,' she said, and they came. Brown hens and white hens, and hens of a freckled white like city dust on snow.

They came long-necked, alert with greed; their stump wings helping in a fret of sound. They came from the secret places of the orchard, jealous for the gold which she threw like rain.

She had corn in her apron. A corner of her apron was lifted and fastened across her body at the hip. In this cradle she had corn, and in the corn her fingers moved; feeling the crawl of it and the firm, shaped goodness.

She brought out her hand; and where her fingers closed small drops of corn squeezed out, as though her fist were a fruit bursting with its seeds. Then she threw the corn among the dedicated heads, and some of it fell on their warm, broad backs.

She looked away to the leaning trees; calling 'Cooop, cooop,' and louder; for one of her brood was missing. She had not counted them, but she knew. The big brown pullet was missing; and she hoped that this meant the big brown pullet was hidden somewhere, doing its best to lay. She was relieved that the big brown pullet knew enough to try.

She thought it a very stupid pullet. She hoped it would learn from the little red hen; which laid without fuss. Or from the fat white hen which laid with passionate efficiency. Or from the speckledy hen which discussed every egg and boasted. She hoped the big brown pullet would learn not to lay at meal times.

Suddenly the big brown pullet came running; startled to be late, and full of fluster. 'Cooop, cooop,' she said, throwing out the rain.

The big brown pullet did not understand. It squawked from the hard rain, then plunged among the others. The little red hen pecked it away. So did the fat white hen and the speckledy. They despised this big brown pullet and were cruel to it.

'Cooop, cooop,' she said, consolingly. She watched its back where the sun poured in the colours. There were reds in the brown feathers; a hidden red as in the chestnut shine. There was the brown of filberts, and the burn of cinnamon; and in its tail feathers there was black, like old burns which have forgotten their flame. She could see the big brown pullet growing beautiful as she watched. She could feel its colours responding to the call out of the sun.

The older hens, made wise by habit, looked up and waited; their eyes the colour of wine when it is firelit in a glass. They waited for more, knowing there would be more; that she would give them more by releasing the corner of her apron and letting them fall in a rain.

She yielded to their waiting, letting the corner of her apron go down and watching the red-crested heads bob around her feet and between. Their beaks knew that she would not move; that her shoes, splintered in the skin like an old smile, were shoes which would stay still.

'Cooop, cooop,' she said, not calling but quietly; her wordless word a part of the quiet. She stood a long time; feeling the peace, the hard brown earth and sun-dry grass, feeling the sun-pattern through the trees.

Then she turned and went calmly down the path; leaving the hens to their litter, to their look-up and look-down day. She did not keep hens for their eggs only. She kept them also for this time of day; when peace came around and bowed its head and saw beauty hidden in the shine of feathers.

GC

160

# Morning Milk

A lantern crosses the farmyard stones. The stones are swollen, like the top crust of a loaf.

Boots come with the lantern; hob-nailed boots as though worn by a man. But they are not. They are worn by Rose, the farmer's daughter, whose job it is to milk four cows while the morning is still blind.

She passes into the shippon and the lantern throws patterns over rumps which will be toffee-coloured by day, but are the colour of beer in this goblin light.

A thin black cat creeps after her, and near the door two kittens box, their eyes bright with trust while the old cat slinks in hope. Rose does not speak to them. She speaks to Daisy the cow, and Daisy moves sideways; made obedient by habit.

Rose puts down her stool, then sits, bucket tilted between her thighs. Her woollen cap rests against the breathing side, and her hands draw to the bucket sounds which are as new as sunlight, as gay as music; calling down a rhythm so steady that she seems to sleep, only her hands awake.

Meanwhile the old cat creeps nearer, and the kittens peer around the wall; their ears pricked, their eyes reflecting the lamplight and full of stares.

*GC*

# Cart Mare

Out of the smoke of November twilight comes the mare; slow and steady, as willing as a priest.

She pulls a cart, and in the cart are mangels. Each mangel is a thing of colours; a purple green on the shoulder which has bulged above ground, as though the cold has pressed it and bruised it. In the belly it is yellow, like the heart of a fire which is prickling quietly into ash; and at the tip, which has found the heart of the earth, there is red as though of blood.

The cart has a smell of raw mangel and moist earth. The smell of the horse is tired.

A man sits on a shaft, his great boots dangling, his hands seamed with earth; black rims of it beneath hands that flinch from nothing, so unfeeling are they, like horn.

He has a hessian sack around his shoulders, a wet cap on the back of his head. He holds the reins, but he is not driving. He knows that the mare cannot be hustled; that she is as firmly grooved as he in the habit called work.

They are as one; this man, this horse, this cart. They come like time down the hill of day.

GC

162

# The Settle and the Screen

Snow is foreign, and speaks in silence its religion of denial. A denial of night, so that the darkness becomes the lost-light. A denial of song, so that the birds are still. A denial of colours, too.

We know the world to be green and brown and red and gold and busy; but the foreigner makes the world a skull, with pain alive in its eyeholes.

Between snow and sky, never moving, never betraying the urgency or courage of life, hangs the crippling cold. It doesn't attack. It doesn't bluster. Only does it persist, until the persistence is an ache. Men flap their arms and console their hands; talking to their shivers and bidding them be still. Think of the fires to come.

The whole of evening is gathered around its fire; as a medieval court was gathered around its king. And when a log is added, thrown on with booted heel to press it deeper, the sparks go up like celebration; defying the cold which would come down the chimney if it dared.

Years ago, two generations and more, when winter was darkness and there was nothing you did not make yourself, years ago the country family shut out winter in two ways.

The settle was drawn forward. It turned its broad, brown back to winter, to the cold which cried in the silence, and pretended that nothing mattered except the court of king fire. It laughed with reflected flames and took on windows of light that peered beyond February to the colours of summer dancing. It held the family in its arms, as though all were children and it a parent, in whom they could have trust. It would protect, it seemed to say; and in its brown embrace father smoked his evening pipe, and mother put her darning fist into another hole. Daughter Jane sang to the firelight; happy songs when the sparks were bright, melancholy when the embers blinked. And brother Bill said nothing in sweet silence, for he had neighbour Jill beside him, and he and Jill were courting.

163

Sometimes they all sang and the settle then was merrier than ever; hugging them and begging, for this was its hour and must go on and on, the best hour of the day.

Then, when the yellow clock yawned, governed by habit like a bore, the settle leaned closer and whispered imaginative stories, so that its family saw pictures in the firelight and refused to believe what the clock plainly said. Minutes were stolen and they were the best; and only when father coughed, put his hands on knees and said, 'Aw, well...,' only then did the settle admit that its hour was done and release them and watch them go and keep their memory warm for as long as the fire survived.

Soon the fire slept, but the settle never did. All night it stood upright, refusing to give the foreigner best though it couldn't do much alone. So the cold came in, and laughed at the fire, spreading its white breath until the kitchen froze. It conquered all in the hours between bedtime and midnight; but it did not conquer the settle which refused to move or shiver or flinch. All night it stood; holding its hands to a fire long dead.

Then there was the family screen; a folding affair which opened wings wide and high so that peer though it might and fret though it might, the cold could not get through.

The screen gathered around the fire, shepherding its people nearer and closer, so that flames were reflected in watching faces and danced like merriment in watching eyes.

It was a motherly screen, telling stories in pictures for those who were young enough to hear the tongues of wonder in pictures told in colour. The whole of this screen was covered with pictures; pasted years ago, nobody knew when.

There were hunting horses jumping, over the hedges to nowhere; fine action studies, with men stern and red and dashing, the women pale and serene. Their eyebrows were always thick and straight, and their hands on the reins were as small as petals.

There were ships at sea and better still, half a ship; a wreck not yet completed, with frightened faces shouting in the green and white-lisp sea. There were pretty maiden faces, wearing hats big and fat like Christmas cakes. There were football teams as fierce as dragoons, with moustaches military and knickerbockers tight. There

164

were uniforms and peacocks, gay and pretty children laughing on a sleigh; and there were highwaymen escaping to the listening stars.

Sometimes a boy said, pointing to the drowning, 'Granma, what ship's that, Granma?' And the smiling voice replied: 'Just a ship, nobody ever knew its name.' And a voyage was on; the boy facing the screen and watching, sailing his ship around the world, while the fire purred like a cat well-stroked, and the foreigner waited.

Then, when the clock spoke as clocks always do, the old woman brought a basin of warm water to the firelight, washing the boy for bed, doing it mildly, not washing away the greatest voyage in the world. And when he wore a nightgown already warmed by the fire's kind breath, she held him on her knee and sang old songs and looked at him and wished that childhood could go on for ever.

Later, when the boy was in bed and the voyage was a sleeping dream, she sat alone within the screen, leaning forward and saying nothing, for the old know how to say it. So the evening moved gently down the quiet of hours until the clock spoke again, and the cold knew its time was coming.

Then the old woman rose and put away her evening when she put away her screen. Suddenly the kitchen was hostile, all hearthside magic lost. And the old woman spoke to the cold, saying, 'Oh, dear, how long are you going to last?' And the cold jabbered that foreign silence which none can understand.

Emmy and Fred have a screen like this. In summer it's folded in a bedroom; leaning against a wall and neglected, even derided as a heavy ole thing, blimmin' old noosance, really. But each winter it comes downstairs to service; and when I called on them last week, they were living within it, shut in with their fire.

Fred moved his feet in the hearth, so that I could put mine there, too. And when they talked about the snow and ice, it seemed that the weather belonged to others for it had no part of this kingdom by the fire.

They told me about their screen; ages old; remembered by Fred from his boyhood, when the evening ale went into the shoe, and the copper shoe went into the fire. They drank hot ale on the eve of bed; father and mother, and the children, too; and the ale and the firelight drowsed them, so that they didn't know the blankets were thin nor heed the foreigner breathing at the window.

A generation later Fred's children came within the screen; standing in the bath on bath-nights, watching the pictures and saying, 'Tell us about that one, Dad.' So Fred said, soaping the flannel while the water chimed warmly down, 'What wan, me dear?' playing for time and trying to remember what he'd said last week. Then he told them about Grace Darling who rowed when the seas were high; hearing the cries of drowning men and begging her father to pull on, pull harder, to pull into the firelight of evening legend. He made the story last until the last flannel was screwed, the last ear explored.

Then, during the towelling, while he hissed as he hissed to the horses, the children would say, 'Tell us about this one, Dad,' taking their pick from the heroes and heroines who lived on the winter screen. And this one would be a soldier, formidable in red and gold, with a sword in defence of the Queen, and a moustache and expression to go with it. Daughter Mary would say: 'Is that you, Dad?' And Emmy would sniff and Fred would say, looking down: 'Naw, tidn yer Dad, tis a chap I used to knaw, handsome gert chap, brave's tiger and I'll tell e fer why...' Then he would make it up as he went along; making it strong because of the listening eyes.

So the screen would show its most exciting pictures until all the children had passed from firelight to bed. Then its colours would pale, and it would be content to watch over the parents as they lived the quietest hour of the day.

Now these screens are few, and the settle is no more. Why? I wonder why.

*SDJ*

166

# A Voice the Colour of Lavender

Long years ago, when song was born in country kitchens and did not come broadcast from an offensive little box, the long pale evenings of summer and the long wagging evenings of winter were friendly with fireside singing. The mother sang to her cradle, her black boot moving and the cradle creaking. And the grandmother sang to her children; her songs as old as the hills, remembered from her childhood and never written down.

I remember the fireside scene of long ago; when my grandmother sat in the corner and leaned forward, so that the flames were in her face. Her eyes were dim, but it seemed to me that always they were smiling; as though they saw beyond the day to some distant land where all was rest and ease, all a long and gentle intimacy.

I remember, and as I remember, I hear again the scratch of rain at the winter window; feel the cold sneaking slit-eyed. Instinctively I go towards the fire, towards the black-gowned person who sits in the corner there; and memory says the fire is huge, the settle high, that her voice is the colour of lavender as she sings.

SDJ

# Poet in the Pub

The boilermaker is a mixture of brown ale and beer. It was the dark preference of Dylan Thomas; the Welsh poet who died young and tragically, with none knowing what he might have attained on the foundation of achievement.

Sound radio and television have not been remarkable for their advancements of writing talent; for the BBC flinches from the new, mistrusting life when it does not wear a white collar. Yet it did much for Dylan Thomas and that's remarkable; for this young man was old in iniquities, not to be relied upon to treat the microphone with that sober deference which the BBC prefers and to which it is accustomed.

It's been said that English writing produced nothing of enduring value between Eliot and Osborne; but that's to forget Dylan Thomas, whose *Under Milk Wood* had an influence comparable to but greater than *The Lady's Not For Burning* and the larger Fry.

I have never been able to reconcile Thomas with the BBC; for he was no refined poet of the Rupert Brook school. He drank. Moreover he boozed. Barmaids were among his best friends; and when he went from the 'seashaken house on a breakneck of rocks' to America, he knew more bartenders than professors, with egg-in-brandy his favourite breakfast.

America tried to make him a celebrity; and although he enjoyed the novelty of acclaim, he seems to have walked down dark streets of chronic despair. He came back to his brambled garden, to his wooden shack by the sea; there to write on a diet of beer, dragging the words by their roots and shouting with the pain. He worked without observable method; writing, for instance, two hundred versions of the poem 'Fern Hill.'

He began some poems with a phrase; which hatched the next, which hatched the next and so on. Sometimes he began only with one word; finding it as productive as a seed. The result could not be reconciled to the beginning; any more than the flower can be seen in the seed.

Much has been said and written about poems: should they be read or heard? Do they deserve the importance and the chains of print? Thomas had a theory that the printed page is the place to examine the words of a poem; with the lecture-platform the place to give it the works.

He has been called a man without religion; without belief in a god. Yet I remember reading how once he defined his poet's purpose: 'To write poems in praise of God's world.' Then he roared down the Welsh hill to his poet's pub.

*SDJ*

# Advice to the Tired

Advice to the tired, the fretful, the fed up; go to a library, any library, and there mooch among the books.

The books will help. The picking down, the flicking through with the freedom to reject; this will do much for bruised or soured vanity. The finding of a book alight with interest but on the bottom shelf, this will reward and delight and put a glow in November chill.

*SDJ*


# Respect for all Life

From 'a fictional diary of one who lived on Dartmoor in the days of long winters and hard brown labour. It recalls the days when Dartmoor was isolated, keeping its own secrets and telling its own story to the listening firelight.'

'I look to the day when all life will be respected; when all who feel as I do will work for the safety and protection of the vulnerable. They will be maligned and mocked and derided as sentimentalists. But they will be feared, not because they are powerful but because cruelty is its own enemy. Perhaps a hundred years from now it will be much better.'

*SDJ*

# A Fag for Christmas

*I can think of only a couple of adult photographs in which Vian does not have a fag in his mouth ('Vian smoked fags, not cigarettes,' as his old newspaper colleague told me). He knew he smoked too much - 'up to forty cigarettes a day, well-thumbed pipes as well' - and tried to give up occasionally, but found that without smoking he couldn't write. Which brings us neatly to a short piece he wrote one Christmas for 'Woman's Realm,' which introduced it thus:*

'Vian Smith is a particular *Realm* favourite who delights our readers with his short stories and articles about the Westcountry, where he lives. The Christmas he best remembers has nothing to do with tinsel or with turkeys. And it happened twenty five years ago...'

It was during the war. We were guarding something obscure in the middle of nowhere. No tea, no mail, apparently no cigarettes. But I had one. It was my secret. I thought myself clever to have saved one. It would be my Christmas.

I sneaked away and brought it out, smoothing the wrinkles, preparing to make it last. I looked for matches. They were wet. They were stupid and would not strike. I kept striking until there were no more, tasting despair because I was a poor soldier who couldn't have a cigarette for Christmas.

I hid it and came back to a colleague, who wasn't a friend, only a uniform. We crouched and shivered and thought of home. The colleague who wasn't a friend, not even a name I can remember, brought out a crumpled packet. One cigarette was in it. He hesitated, broke it carefully, holding out half despite my look away. He shielded the match and lit mine first. We didn't speak. We smoked - deeply.

He was ten years older than I. It's the only excuse I can offer. I've never thanked him but I do so now, because he taught me what Christmas is all about.

# Published Works of Vian Smith

Novels by Vian C. Smith published by Hodder and Stoughton

*Song of the Unsung* 1945
*Candles to the Dawn* 1946
*Hungry Waters* 1948
*The Hand of the Wind* 1948
*Holiday for Laughter* 1949
*So Many Worlds* 1950
*Stars in the Morning* 1950


Novels by Vian Smith published by Peter Davies

*Question Mark* 1961 (US title *Pride of the Moor*, Doubleday)
*Press Gang* 1961
*Genesis Down* 1962
*The First Thunder* 1966
*The Wind Blows Free* 1968
*Minstrel Boy* 1970


Novels for Young Readers published in the UK by Longmans and in the USA by Doubleday

*Martin Rides the Moor* 1964
*Green Heart* 1964 (US publication only)
*The Horses of Petrock* 1965 (US title *A Second Chance*)
*King Sam* 1966 (US title *Tall and Proud*)
*Come Down the Mountain* 1967
*The Lord Mayor's Show* 1968
*Moon in the River* 1969

## Non-Fiction

*Portrait of Dartmoor* 1966 (Hale)
*A Horse Called Freddie* 1967 (Stanley Paul)
*Point to Point* 1968 (Stanley Paul)
*The Grand National* 1969 (Stanley Paul)

## Non-Fiction for Young Readers

*Vian Smith's Parade of Horses* 1970 (Longmans)
(US title *Horses in the Green Valley*, Doubleday)

## Radio Plays (broadcast by the BBC)

*Green Heart*
*The White Stallion*
*Saturday Morning on the Hill*
*The Boy Who Made It*
*Inherit the Earth*

## Television Plays (shown on ITV)

*The First Thunder*
*Giants on Saturday*

## Guides

*Dittisham Pocket Souvenir* 1949 (no publisher given)
*Totnes Official Guide* c1949
*Bovey Tracey Official Guide* c1965 (Editor)

# Subscribers

*The Longmarsh Press gratefully acknowledges the following who, in subscribing to this book in advance, helped to facilitate its publication:*

Kathy and Rob Alexander
Amanda and Felipe d'Ayala
Kate Campbell
Pat Coke
Will and Gina Coles
David Cutts
Mark Lindsey Earley, Grand Bard of Exeter
Rod Edwards
Pamela Forbes
Len Gammon
Laurence Green
Tom and Elisabeth Greeves, Tavistock
James Gresham
Colin Hair
Deborah Harvey
George Holland Hill
Philip and Anne Hodder
Dave George Holland
Kitty Jay
Cathy and Peter Kiddle
Jane Lepine Smith
Gwyneth Lorimer
Kevin Marman
Anne Mattock
Alan Miles
Jan and Elizabeth Morris
Kim Morris
Helen Nelder
David Phillips (TIP)
E. Plain
Ken Prout

Peter Rees
Ring o' Bells, North Bovey
Graham Rutherford
Allen Saddler
Tom Sheppard
Tony and Caroline Stilwell
Colin and Cilla Turner
Marcia and Roddy Willett
Carole Wills

### The Longmarsh Press

The Longmarsh Press was founded in 2008 by Totnes writer Bob Mann, initially to publish books covering Devon history, topography, culture and tradition, as well as books by Devon writers, past and present, but other subjects may be included as well. It takes its name from the mile-long reclaimed area by the River Dart on the Bridgetown side of Totnes.

If you have any ideas or suggestion please contact the Longmarsh Press at 5 Brook View, Follaton, Totnes TQ9 5FH, 01803 847930; bobmann@supanet.com

It is hoped that the following titles will appear in 2009:

*Totnes on the Dart* Bob Mann
*The Totnes Ghost Book* Bob Mann and Mark Lindsey Earley
*Writers in the Devon Landscape* Bob Mann
*A Richer Dust: Who's Buried Where in Devon* Bob Mann

Born in Totnes in 1958, Bob Mann is well known as a writer, speaker and walks guide whose work covers the history, folklore, creative associations and psychogeography of the town and surrounding area. He has published guides, histories, topographical portraits of places, stories and countless articles and reviews.